SENECA

SENECA.

From the double bust of Seneca and Socrates in
the Berlin Museum.

SENECA

BY

FRANCIS ⌐HOLLAND

WITH FRONTISPIECE

Select Bibliographies Reprint Series

BOOKS FOR LIBRARIES PRESS
FREEPORT, NEW YORK

First Published 1920
Reprinted 1969

STANDARD BOOK NUMBER:
8369-5131-X

LIBRARY OF CONGRESS CATALOG CARD NUMBER:
72-102246

PRINTED IN THE UNITED STATES OF AMERICA

INTRODUCTORY NOTE

THIS essay in biography was originally intended as an introduction to a translation of Seneca's letters, the greater part of which has been completed. But as this translation is not likely ever to be published, I have decided, after long hesitation, to print the introduction by itself, on the chance that here or there some reader may be found to share my interest in the subject.

Of the three branches into which philosophy, in the ancient view, divided itself—ethic, physic, and logic—it is with the two first alone that Seneca was concerned. He never lost touch with life and reality. To those who ' love to lose themselves in a mystery,' and rest in an ' O Altitudo ! ' Seneca as a philosopher makes no appeal. Rather would he teach men how to find themselves and, so far as is possible to souls closed in by a ' vesture of decay,' to understand the meaning of life and of death. His meaning is never ambiguous. However shallow a pool may be, as has often been said, you cannot see to the bottom if the water is muddy. Like the waters of the Lake of Garda, on the other hand, Seneca's thoughts combine clearness with depth. He played too large a part in a critical period of history and of thought to find time for the abstract speculations and dialectical subtleties with which the logical branch of philosophy was concerned, and in which the Greek masters of the Stoic school were mainly interested; and no doubt it is this *esprit positif* which so commended him to his great debtor, Montaigne.

I have added, 'to fill the page,' a paper on Caius Maecenas, which appeared long ago in the *Dublin Review*. I have to thank the editor for the permission to republish, which has not been refused.

CONTENTS

to p. 63

SENECA

CHAPTER I

MARCUS ANNAEUS SENECA AND HIS SONS—THE
CONTROVERSIAE—HELVIA — THE BATTLE OF
THE BOOKS

A PLEASANT impression of the tranquil old age
of Marcus Annaeus Seneca, the father of the
philosopher, under the principate of Tiberius,
is given in the dedications to his three sons,
Novatus, Lucius Seneca, and Mela,[1] which are pre-
fixed to his five books of *Controversiae*. These
Controversiae, which first came into fashion in
the time of Cicero,[2] were imaginary cases argued
on one side and the other by the professors in
the schools of rhetoric for the instruction of their
pupils, or by the pupils in the presence and
under the direction of their masters. They turned
on disputable questions of ethics or law — a

---

[1] ' Docti Senecae ter numeranda domus ' (Martial, iv. 40).

[2] *Dialog. de Orat.* 35. Before the age of Cicero general
questions were discussed in the schools as theses, in Cicero's
time these became *causae*, and were modelled on the actual cases
tried in the courts, and these in their turn were succeeded by
the *controversiae*, which came to hold, as the form through which
eloquence was taught, the chief place in the education of the
young Roman (Seneca, *Controv.* i. Pref.).

non-existent rule of law being generally assumed for the purpose of the pleadings—and the more dramatic and improbable the circumstances imagined by the rhetoricians, the more crowded with pupils were their schools, and the greater their consequent renown.[1]

In the great days of the republic, when the sovereign power at Rome was vested ultimately in the various assemblies of her citizens, the faculty of swaying these assemblies by eloquence was almost the one necessary qualification for a successful career, yet it was not till the generation immediately preceding the establishment of the Empire that the art of rhetoric was taught systematically at Rome. Before that time a youth who looked forward to a forensic career would be introduced by his father to one of the celebrated orators of the day, whose methods he would study, whose pleadings he would never fail to attend, and to whom he would render

[1] Tyrants and pirates were favourite characters in these declamations—tyrants who issue edicts ordering sons to execute their fathers, pirates with lovely daughters who rescue and elope with their father's prisoners. The art is to involve the actors on either side in a conflict between equally sacred obligations. In their beginnings, however, in the time recalled by the elder Seneca, the *controversiae* were less extravagant and more nearly related to reality. Thus in a controversy declaimed before the Emperor Augustus with Agrippa and Maecenas in attendance, in which Marcus Seneca's chief friend, Porcius Latro, was the principal interlocutor, the case supposed relates to a father of two sons, one of whom he had disinherited. The disinherited son forms a connection with a woman who bears him a son. On his death-bed he sends the woman to his father, and commends to him his son. The father adopts the boy. The other son disputes this arrangement, and pleads that his father is not of sound mind or capable of making such a disposition. The case is argued between them.

what assistance he could.[1] When rhetoric was first studied in Rome as an art, and for the training just described was substituted that of the schools, the *causae* there discussed were made to resemble as closely as possible the cases of the forum—the one bearing to the other the same sort of relation that the proceedings in political debating societies bear to the debates in the House of Commons. But after the fall of the republic, when the orators who had numbered kings and nations among their clients, or had impeached proconsuls for the oppression of provinces, were succeeded by the *delatores*, who earned fame, indeed, and vast sums of money, but also the detestation of all honest men by bringing accusations against great senators whom the emperors wished to destroy,[2] the rhetorical exercises of the schools became ever more and more remote from reality. The object of teachers and pupils alike was not to bring conviction to the minds of their hearers, but to win applause for their own cleverness. Rhetoric ceased to have an object outside itself—it became an art for art's sake. The triumph of the controversialists in these fantastic contests was the

[1] The next step for an ambitious youth was the impeachment of some great State offender. Thus Julius Caesar in his twenty-first year impeached Dolabella, and Asinius Pollio at about the same age became famous by his prosecution of Cato.

[2] The State having become, as it were, personified in the emperor, the prosecution of the victims of imperial tyranny appeared to the prosecutors to be of the same nature as the famous impeachments of republican times, and an orator such as Memmius Regulus, while serving as the instrument of a Domitian's cruelty, would regard himself as a Cicero accusing Verres.

invention of the effective aphorisms, antitheses, or epigrams called *sententiae*, which were applauded for their pithiness or ingenuity, and easily retained in the memory. ' Knowledge is the foundation of eloquence '—'*rem tene, verba sequentur,*' wrote the elder Cato in the earliest Roman treatise on oratory. The rhetoricians of the schools seemed to reverse this maxim, and to believe eloquence to be the foundation of knowledge—so all-important a place did rhetoric hold in the later Roman scheme of education, and so remote from the real business of life and of the forum had their rhetorical exercises become. No one, as Tacitus wrote, in republican times attained great power without the aid of eloquence. Consequently, the attainment of linguistic mastery of expression was the chief aim of education, and so continued to be after the establishment of the Empire. In the grammatical course, which preceded that of rhetoric, boys were trained through the medium of classical poetry.

Marcus Annaeus Seneca is himself generally described in modern books as a rhetorician; but although he was intimate with the greatest masters of the art, attended their lectures and declamations with assiduity, and treasured their *sententiae* in his memory, there is no direct evidence that he himself ever taught in the schools. He came to Rome from his native Corduba in Spain as soon as the close of the civil wars allowed him to leave that colony, afterwards regretting that he had not been able to come sooner, since then he might have heard the living voice of Cicero—an epithet commonly used, he adds, but to the voice of Cicero really applicable.[1]

His collection of *Controversiae* was made at the request of his sons who, anxious to know something of the character and style of the famous rhetors of the preceding generation, begged their father to tell them all he could remember on the subject. His memory had been famous in the days of his youth; and we cannot wonder that it was esteemed a prodigy if we may believe his assurance that he was then able to repeat without an error two thousand names in the right order after a single hearing. But in his old age, he adds, it had become capricious; he could no longer count on its ready and immediate obedience to his will, but was obliged to wait its pleasure. For the events of his youth it was as strong as ever, but it could not retain what was in later years entrusted to its keeping; just as in a vessel already filled to which more water is added what is on the surface overflows and is lost, but what is below remains. He applauds the desire of his sons to learn

---

[1] Cicero, after Julius Caesar's final victories had silenced his voice in the forum, amused himself by giving lessons in declamation to Hirtius and Dolabella—two of the most distinguished of Caesar's officers—on their return from the war. These great pupils of his—'grandes praetextatos' he calls them—were at that time compensating themselves for the fatigues of their campaigns by a life of pleasure at Rome. 'They were my masters,' said Cicero, 'in the art of dining, as I was theirs in the art of speaking' (Cicero, *Ep.* ix. 16 ; Suet. *de claris Rhet.*). This was in the year 46 B.C. If Marcus Seneca was fifteen or sixteen years of age at the time, he would have been born about the year 61 B.C. (Sen. *Controv.* i. Pref.).

something of the eloquence of the past generation
—in the first place, because the more numerous
and various the models before them the less are
they likely to become mere imitators ; and, in
the second place, because the age is degenerate,
and because the art of rhetoric having reached
its height about the time of Cicero had, according to the universal law of change, been declining ever since. In the days of freedom, so
he continues, rhetorical exercises had a serious
object, since by eloquence a man might reach
the highest offices of the State ; but, since the
overthrow of the republic, this spur to effort
had largely been withdrawn. He had heard all
the great orators except Cicero, and the task
of satisfying the praiseworthy curiosity of his
sons by returning as it were to school in his old
age, and bringing to light out of the caverns of
his memory all that they contained of the declamations made in the schools by the celebrated
rhetoricians of the past, would be to him a delightful labour. The publication of their witty
sayings and ingenious subtleties would also in-
cidentally have the useful effect of checking the
unacknowledged plagiarisms of their degenerate
successors.

The elder Seneca was a Roman of the old
school, of equestrian rank, a lover of the past—
orderly, austere, and methodical. His wife, Helvia,
belonged to an influential provincial family,
in which a severe simplicity was a tradition.[1]

[1] 'Bene in antiqua et severa institutam domo' (*Cons. ad Helv.* xvi.).

Like most mothers of distinguished men she was, if we may accept the description left of her by her son the philosopher, a woman of remarkable character and intelligence. Her husband, to whom any departure from old Roman customs and ideas was distasteful,[1] was opposed to what we now call the higher education of women, and would not suffer her to devote much time to study, a circumstance regretted by her son, in whose judgment there were few on whom such opportunities would have been less likely to be wasted, or who in the little time actually allowed could have acquired so much. He tells us that his mother took deep interest in his philosophical studies, while her delight in his society was inexhaustible; and, on the other hand, that the very sight of her always filled him with an almost boyish gaiety and gladness. After her widowhood, which succeeded within thirty days the death of the kindest of brothers, she administered with the utmost care and disinterestedness the inheritance of her three sons; refusing all personal advantage from it as if it had been another's, and giving as much care to its management as if it had been her own. In the same way the course of honours which two of her sons successfully pursued, and the fortunes they acquired, though giving her pleasure for their sake, were a source not of profit to herself, but of additional expense—so much better did she deem it to give than to receive.

Novatus, the eldest of the three sons of Marcus

[1] ' Nimis majorum consuetudini deditus ' (*Cons. ad Helv.* xvi.).

Seneca and Helvia, was adopted by his father's friend, Junius Gallio the rhetorician, by whose name he became known. He entered early on an official career, passing through all the official dignities till he became *consul suffectus*, after which he became Proconsul of Achaia in the year 52, where the accident of a riot, resulting in the appearance of Paul of Tarsus before his tribunal, immortalised a name which all the praises of his brother Seneca, who describes him as the most irresistibly charming man of his age, could not have rescued from oblivion.[1] If we may trust his brother's description, he was indeed a man made to be loved. 'No one man,' writes the younger Seneca, with his usual rhetorical exaggeration, 'is so agreeable to another as Gallio to all who know him'—'*nemo enim mortalium*

[1] The identity of the Gallio of the Acts with Gallio the brother of Seneca is made practically certain by an incidental reference to his brother in Achaia in one of the philosopher's letters to Lucilius : '*Illud mihi in ore erat domini mei Gallionis, qui cum in Achaia febrem habere caepisset, protinus navem adscendit, clamitans non corporis esse, sed loci morbum*' (*Ep.* civ.). Achaia, which comprised all the Peloponnesus and the greater part of Hellas proper with the islands, had been an imperial province under Tiberius and Caligula, but was transferred to the Senate by Claudius in A.D. 44 (Tac. *Ann.* i. 76; Suet. *Claudius*, 25). The date of Gallio's proconsulship (52) has been ascertained by the discovery of an inscription at Delphi containing four fragments of a letter of Claudius to the city. Pliny alludes to a voyage made by Gallio for the sake of his health, which may be the same as that spoken of by Seneca : '*Praeterea est alius usus multiplex, principalis vero navigandi phthisi affectis, ut diximus, aut sanguinem egerentibus : sicut proxime Anneum Gallionem fecisse post Consulatum meminimus*' (Plin. *N.H.* xxxi. 6). Seneca had been recalled from exile in 49, and his brother Gallio must have been *consul suffectus* in 50 or 51. It was the custom of the emperors at that time to nominate consuls for short periods, though the year was named only after those first appointed.

uni tam dulcis est quam hic omnibus.' [1] 'His courtesy and unstudied charm of manner win every heart, yet so modest is he that not only does he shrink from the very approaches of flattery, but listens with equal reluctance to the praises which his numerous excellences have really deserved.' [2]

The youngest brother Mela, to whom the second book of 'Controversies' is exclusively addressed, though described by his father as mentally the best endowed of the three, made an early resolution to content himself with his hereditary rank and, leaving the career of honours to his two accomplished brothers, to devote himself to a life of studious retirement. His father, though he did not conceal his own preference for an active career, acquiesced without much difficulty in this decision, declaring that he was ready, when his two elder sons had put out to sea, to keep the third in harbour. That Mela was his favourite son, and that this lack of ambition was a disappointment to one so enamoured of traditionary ways as the elder Seneca, will seem probable to the reader of the dedication addressed to him; nor would he have been greatly consoled had he been able to foresee that this contempt for the ancient State dignities would not prevent his son from accumulating a large fortune as procurator of the imperial demesne under the principate of Nero.

---

[1] Cf. Statius, *Sylv.* ii. 7: 'Hoc plus quam Senecam dedisse mundo, Aut *dulcem* generâsse Gallionem.'

[2] *Nat. Quaest.* iv. Praef.

The Senecas appear to have been a most united family. But whereas the father held the view common to old men in every age that the era of great men was over, and that in the new generation there was an unexampled dearth of talent and ability in every kind, the sons were believers in progress, with scant respect for authority, tradition, or national feeling.

The reminiscences of the *Controversiae* in which the father endeavours to convince his sons by description and quotation of the superiority of the past generation, were the outcome of this difference of view. In the preface of the last book he declares that they shall trouble him no longer. He owns he is weary of the subject. At first he thought it would be pleasant to summon up remembrance of things past and recall the best years of his life under the mild Augustus, but he now feels half ashamed, as if he attached too much importance to such studies. These exercises of ingenuity, he says, are well enough if taken lightly : take them too seriously and they disgust. He could not admire the modern rhetorician Musa, whom his sons had insisted on his accompanying them to hear. He thinks his style turgid and unnatural, declares the man has no sincerity, and, in spite of Mela's frowning disapproval—' *licet Mela meus contrahat frontem* '—gives instances of what he means from the declamation he had heard. Clearly between father and sons, in spite of high mutual affection and respect, no agreement on these points was reached or possible.

The positions of the various controversialists in the ' battle of the books,' fought in the second half of the first century between the upholders of the classical tradition in writing and speaking and the new school, between ancient and modern ideas and standards, are admirably given in the dialogue *De Oratoribus*, generally ascribed to Tacitus. The dialogue is for all time a model of urbane controversy, in which the most complete difference of opinion is effectively expressed without a trace of acerbity or sarcasm. The views of the author are probably represented by the gentle Maternus, who, after Afer and Messala have pleaded the cause of the moderns and of the ancients respectively, takes a middle course. He admits with Messala the fact of the decay of eloquence, but argues that this is the result of the change in the character of the times and in the nature of the government rather than of any decline in the abilities of men. Augustus, indeed, together with everything else, had pacified eloquence which could only flourish in turbulent times; but he suggests that eloquence was not of such importance that it was desirable that the times should be turbulent in order that it might flourish. He might have added that good art being the true representation of emotion, passion, or thought, which the artist has himself experienced either actually or through sympathy, it must change with the changing life of the day and cannot be limited by old conventions.

Original minds may not force their ideas into an ancient mould on pain of illustrating the couplet of Boileau :

> 'Voulant se redresser soi-même on s'estropie,
> Et d'un original devient une copie.'

When, however, we compare the graceful, easy-flowing style of Livy, Cicero, and Virgil, their avoidance of over-emphasis or abrupt transitions, the rise and fall of their periods, and the even texture of their narrative, comparable to a good mountain road, which is never irksome to a traveller whatever the height to which it rises—when we compare this with the bold realism, the disregard for convention and tradition, the cosmopolitanism, and the striking but often isolated thoughts and aphorisms of Lucan and Tacitus and Juvenal, we can understand the extreme dislike which such admirers of antiquity in later generations as Quintilian or Aulus Gellius or Fronto felt for the younger Seneca, whom they rightly regarded as the chief author of this revolution in taste. The transition resembles, both in its nature and in the circumstance of the intervening revolution, that from the French encyclopaedists of the eighteenth century to Chateaubriand and Victor Hugo—a transition deplored by Sainte-Beuve, who might be called the Quintilian of the nineteenth century.

CHAPTER II

EARLY YEARS AND EDUCATION—SOTION,
ATTALUS, FABIANUS

LUCIUS ANNAEUS SENECA, the second son of
Marcus Seneca and Helvia, was born at Corduba
about the commencement of the Christian era.[1]
He was living at Rome, as we have seen, with
his parents and brothers in the days of Tiberius,
and while still a boy was seized with a passion
for those philosophical studies which were to
be the chief interest of his life and his best title
to fame. His earliest master in philosophy was
Sotion, a native of Alexandria, under whose
influence he ' thought nobly ' for a time of the
doctrines of Pythagoras.

Sotion showed us [he afterwards wrote in a letter to
Lucilius[2]] ' the reasons of Pythagoras and afterwards of
Sextius for abstaining from meat—reasons differing from

[1] ' Quae Tritonide fertiles Athenas
    Unctis, Baetica, provocas trapetis,
    Lucanum potes imputare terris.
    Hoc plus quam Senecam dedisse mundo,
    Aut dulcem generâsse Gallionem.'
                            (Statius, *Sylv*. ii. 7.)
[2] *Ep*. cviii.

one another yet in each case of a high nature. Sextius maintained that man could find food enough in the world without shedding blood, and that the association of the satisfaction of his appetites with the slaughter of beasts was a cause of cruelty. He thought, too, that it was wise to circumscribe as much as possible the raw material of luxury, and, moreover, that a vegetarian diet was best for the health. But Pythagoras believed in the common nature and the inter-communion of all things. Nothing, he thought, that has life can perish; but all things must suffer change and pass in never-ending succession from one form into another. We cannot tell after how many vicissitudes and how many dwelling-places a soul will return into the form of man, but we run the risk of committing murder or even parricide when we slay or devour an animal in which some soul we have known in human shape may be abiding. When Sotion had expounded to us these doctrines of Pythagoras, he would ask us whether we believed that lives passed from one body to another, that what we called death was but transmigration, that the souls of men might inhabit flocks or wild beasts or fishes, that nothing perished in the universe but only changed its place, and that men and animals no less than the heavenly bodies go their appointed rounds and know the same vicissitudes ? ' Great men,' he would add, ' have believed these things, but I do not wish to fetter your judgment concerning them. Yet if they be true you are right to abstain from meat, and if false what harm can you suffer from such abstention ? It is at least a useful economy.' Moved by these considerations I eat no meat for a whole year, and after a very short time found this regimen not only easy but agreeable. My mind seemed lighter and more agile—to this day I cannot affirm with certainty whether it really was so or not. You will wonder why I abandoned this diet. I will explain to you why. My youth was passed under the principate of Tiberius, at a time when foreign rites

were prohibited in Rome.[1] Abstention from the flesh
of certain animals was held to be evidence of an inclination towards the Jewish superstition, and therefore at the request of my father, who was no enemy
to philosophy but feared a scandal, I returned to my
former habits, and he found no difficulty in persuading
me to eat better dinners.[2]

From Sotion the Pythagorèan, the young
Seneca passed to the lecture-room of Attalus
the Stoic, whose influence upon his life and
ideas was of a more decisive character. Attalus
is described by the elder Seneca as by far the
acutest and most eloquent philosopher of his
time—' *magnae vir eloquentiae, ex philosophis,
quos nostra aetas vidit, longe et subtilissimus et
facundissimus.*'[3] We know nothing of his life,
except that, having been cheated of his property
by Sejanus, he consoled himself as a philosopher
should by following the plough ; but we know
something of his mind by the many references to
him and quotations from his sayings to be found
in the works of his admiring pupil, Lucius Seneca.

[1] This edict was issued in the year 19 : ' Actum et de sacris
aegyptiis judaicisque pellendis : factumque patrum consultum,
" ut quatuor millia libertini generis, ea superstitione infecta,
quîs idonea aetas, in insulam Sardiniam veherentur . . . ceteri
cederent Italia, nisi certam ante diem profanos ritus exuissent " '
(Tac. *Ann.* ii. 85).

[2] *Ep.* cviii. The old reading was : ' Patre itaque me rogante,
qui non calumniam timebat, sed philosophiam oderat, ad
pristinam consuetudinem redii,' but it is probable that the
suggested emendation of Lipsius is correct, since we may infer
from the decorous conservatism manifest in the writings of the
elder Seneca that he was unlikely to be indifferent to scandal,
and from his words to Mela—' non sum bonae mentis impedi-
mentum '—that his attitude to philosophy was at least tolerant.

[3] *Suas.* ii.

The young enthusiast besieged, so he tells us, the door of Attalus' classroom ; he was always the first to enter when it was opened, and the last to leave. Nor was this all. Attalus was a man of easy access, most friendly disposed towards his pupils, whose ingenuous advances he was ever ready to meet more than half-way. The young Seneca would walk with him and draw him into discussion on subjects of perennial interest. It was Attalus, he tells us, who taught him to distinguish between reality and appearances, between the eloquence of truth and that of display, between intrinsic beauty and the empty sound of swelling words. He would pour contempt alike on luxury and on avarice ; he would extol a chaste body, a sober table, a mind purified not only from unlawful but even from superfluous pleasures. He told his pupils that those who came to a philosopher's lectures merely as an agreeable way of passing the time, to hear and not to learn, to listen to eloquent phrases and ingenious conceits, without any intention of shaping anew the conduct of their life, would derive no profit from philosophy.

However transitory [Seneca afterwards wrote] might be on many the effect of such exhortations, yet the minds of the young being tender and impressionable, if the master is sincere and solely occupied with the good of his pupils his words will have lasting effects. At all events [he adds] this was true in my case. My admiration for him was boundless, and when I heard him speak of the faults, the errors, and the evils of life, I often was moved with compassion for mankind, and he seemed to me more than human.

Under the influence of this teaching Seneca for a time lived a life of asceticism according to the strictest rule of the Stoics and, though it was not long before he reverted to a more ordinary way of life, there were some habits then contracted and some abstinences then resolved upon which he never abandoned.   In the letter already quoted, written to Lucilius near the end of his life, after describing the teaching of Attalus and his own youthful enthusiasm, he adds :

Something of all this remained with me, Lucilius. After the great original impulse had spent its force, I persevered in some fragments of that high enterprise. Thus I have abstained throughout my life from such delicacies as oysters and mushrooms.   They are not food, but condiments, meant to stimulate a jaded appetite, and the delight of the gluttonous because they are easily swallowed and easily vomited.   So, too, from that time onward I have never used ointment, believing that the best odour for the body is the absence of odour ; never touched wine ; and always avoided hot-air baths.   To boil down the body and exhaust it by sweating always seemed to me a luxurious superfluity.   From other renunciations I desisted ; but I returned to what I had abandoned with a moderation that came much nearer to abstinence than self-indulgence—a moderation perhaps even more difficult in practice than total abstention, for certainly it is often easier to abandon a habit altogether than to keep it within modest bounds.[1]

Another of Seneca's habits, dating probably from this time, which ought to win him some sympathy from Englishmen, was the daily cold

[1] *Ep.* 108.

bath all the year round, for which, as in one of his letters he tells us, he became known :

I, that famous cold-bather (Psychrolutes), who, on the first of January, used to disport myself in the moat; who used to celebrate the coming of the new year by leaping into the water brought down from the hills, just as others would celebrate it by some auspicious words spoken read or written, first transferred my camp to the Tiber, and lastly to this tub of mine which, when I am feeling my strongest and acting in perfect good faith with myself, is heated only by the sun.[1]

Another master, whose memory was ever honoured by Seneca, and by whom at this time he was instructed, was the learned author Papirius Fabianus, an old friend of his father. Fabianus had acquired an early reputation as a rhetorician, having studied rhetoric under Blandus—the first man of equestrian rank to teach that art in Rome.[2]

The elder Seneca describes his style in declamation as easy fluent and rapid, but lacking in vigour and incisiveness. He had succeeded so well, he tells us, in banishing such passions as anger or grief from his own breast that he had lost the power of representing them; and this in a rhetorician was a defect. But his critic had not long the opportunity of hearing him, for Fabianus soon transferred his allegiance from rhetoric to philosophy and natural science, and it was as a

---

[1] *Ep.* 83.
[2] Until that time the teaching of rhetoric had been confined to freedmen. The elder Seneca, in stating this, expresses his wonder that it should at any time have been considered dishonouring to teach what by universal admission it was honourable to learn.

philosopher that he contributed to the education
of the younger Seneca.[1]

Fabianus was a copious author. His works are
frequently cited by Pliny in the *Natural History*,
and Lucius Seneca says of his philosophical
writings that they were surpassed only by those
of Cicero, Pollio, and Livy. He wrote in a level
style and with a certain carelessness of diction
that seemed to prove him more occupied with
his matter than his manner. 'Too much attention to style,' replied Seneca to his correspondent
Lucilius who had read on his recommendation a
book of Fabianus and been much disappointed,
'does not become a philosopher who should be
thinking of more important matters. How can
a man defy fortune if he is nervous about words ?
Had you heard him, as I did, your admiration
for the whole would have left you no leisure to
criticise the parts. What though the calm progress
of his discourse was interspersed by no sudden and
striking reflections (" *subiti ictus sententiarum* "),
the very evenness of its flow had a charm of its own.
There was nothing laboured about his eloquence ;
it accompanied him like a shadow without any
effort on his part. You could see that he felt
what he said or wrote; that his object was to
show you what he admired and not to excite your
admiration for himself. He was not slovenly

---

[1] Even after he had formally abandoned rhetoric for
philosophy he continued to study eloquence as a means, though
no longer as an end—his example in this respect being held up
for imitation by Marcus Seneca to his son Mela whom he
endeavoured to convince of the importance of eloquence whatever way of life he might see fit to adopt.

in his use of words, but unconcerned ; his sole interest was the profit of his hearers.' Seneca ends his description by adding that Fabianus' lectures were admirably calculated to elevate the mind of a well-disposed youth and to spur him on to imitate so excellent an example, without causing him to despair of success.[1]

Such were the instructors of the young Seneca under the principate of Tiberius. His health throughout life was delicate. While still young he was brought to great misery by an affection of the lungs, which he calls *suspirium*.[2]

Wasted to a shadow [he afterwards wrote], I was often tempted to cut short my life, but the old age of the kindest of fathers still held me back. I reflected that I ought to consider not so much with what fortitude I could die, but how impossible it was that he could bear my loss with fortitude. Therefore I bade myself live ; for there are times when it is a mark of courage even to live. I will tell you what were then my consolations, observing first that these were also the most useful of medicines, for certain it is that whatever elevates the soul does good to the body. My studies saved me. It was to Philosophy that I owed the power to rise from my bed and the recovery of my health—and this is the least of my obligations to her. My friends watched with me : their encouragements and their conversation contributed much to my restoration. There is nothing, my dearest Lucilius, like the affection of friends to assist and renew a sick man ; nothing that so certainly beguiles us from the expectation and the fear of death.[3]

[1] *Ep.* 100.
[2] ' Satis enim apte dici suspirium potest. Brevis autem valde, et procellae similis, impetus est : intra horam fere desinit' (*Ep.* liv.).
[3] *Ep.* 78.

Through several of his illnesses, and probably through this one, Seneca was nursed by his aunt—a half-sister of Helvia and the widow of Vetrasius Pollio, for sixteen years governor of Egypt under Tiberius.[1] It was she who had brought him as a child from Spain to Rome; and he regarded her with especial admiration and respect. He relates in her honour an incident of which he was himself a witness. Her husband died at sea; there was a storm; the ship's tackle was destroyed and the ship in great danger; the only thought of the widow was for her husband's body from which no danger could separate her and which she succeeded in saving. At a later date, though naturally modest and retiring with a dislike of publicity of any kind that stood out in strong contrast to the general tone of the fashionable women of her time, she exerted all her influence to obtain for her nephew the quaestorship and became, as he wrote to his mother, ambitious for his sake.[2]

Towards the end of the principate of Tiberius, Lucius Seneca, at the desire of his father, abandoned for a time the schools of philosophy and practised with success at the Bar. This was the usual beginning for those who were ambitious to succeed in an official career and to raise themselves through the various ascending

---

[1].It was the custom of Tiberius to continue in their civil and military governments and offices for long periods of years, and sometimes for life, those whom he thought worthy of his confidence.

[2] *Consol. ad Helviam.*

magistracies to senatorial rank and the government of provinces.

Your brothers [the elder Seneca wrote to Mela] are ambitious ; and are preparing themselves for a career in the forum and in office in which even success has its dangers. Time was when I myself longed for and applauded such a career; and, dangerous though it be, I have urged your brothers to pursue it, so far at least as they can do so within the strictest limits of honour.[1]

That the temptations to overstep these limits in the closing years of Tiberius were numerous may be inferred from the short description left us by Seneca of the time—a description by a disinterested eye-witness with no anti-imperial prejudices which the defenders of that emperor find it more difficult to explain away than the invectives of later writers.

Under Tiberius [he wrote] there grew up a frenzied passion for bringing accusations which increased till it became almost universal and proved more destructive to citizens than any civil war. Words spoken by men when drunk and the most harmless pleasantries were denounced. There was safety nowhere ; any pretext was good enough to serve for an information. Nor, after a time, did the accused think it worth while to await the result of their trials, for this was always the same.[2]

There had never been a public prosecutor in Rome ; it had been of old the duty of citizens to keep watch over one another in the interests of the republic; and for the republic was after-

---

[1] Seneca, *Controv*. ii. Praef.
[2] *De Benef*. iii. 16.

wards substituted the emperor. To bring a charge under the law of *majestas*, in the presumed interest of the emperor, had become the quickest road to forensic distinction and a fortune. It is to the credit of Seneca that, unlike Silius Italicus and many others, he remembered his father's proviso with regard to honour and was innocent of this kind of impeachment.

CHAPTER III

WE know little of the life of Seneca during the closing years of Tiberius and the principate of Caligula. Tiberius died in 37, and the elder Seneca at a great age some years earlier, probably in Spain, as his three sons were absent from his death-bed[1] and we know that his widow administered with care and sagacity their rich inheritance. Writing in the first year of Claudius, the younger Seneca speaks of the money reputation and honours lavishly bestowed on him by fortune of which exile had deprived him and of the public honours earned by the industry of his brother Gallio. For these distinctions the philosophical Mela had scorned to compete; but he too is spoken of as wealthy.[2] Seneca was married and the father of a boy, whom he thus described to his mother :

[1] 'Carissimum virum, ex quo mater trium liberorum eras, extulisti. Lugenti tibi luctus nuntiatus est, omnibus quidem absentibus liberis ; quasi de industria in id tempus conjectis malis tuis ut nihil esset ubi se dolor tuus reclinaret ' (*Consol. ad Helv.* ii.). Lucius Seneca wrote a biography of his father with the title *De Vita Patris*. Of this only the fragment of a sentence remains.

[2] His son Lucan was born in the year 39 at Corduba and brought to Rome in 40 when seven months old. The author of the ancient life of Lucan who tells us this says also that Mela was known at Rome through his brother Seneca, ' a man famous for every virtue,' and through his love of a quiet life (' *propter studium vitae quietioris* ').

Marcus, the most winning of children, in whose presence sadness cannot endure. What breast so heavy-laden that his embrace cannot lighten? What wound so fresh that his kisses cannot soothe? What tears can resist his gaiety? What mind so oppressed by care that his nonsense cannot relax? Who can help laughing at his pranks? What brooding meditation so concentrated and absorbed that his delightful chatter cannot interrupt and turn the brooder himself into a fellow-chatterbox? I pray the gods that he may survive me.[1]

Gallio, too, had married and was a widower. His daughter Novatilla was regarded by Seneca almost as a child of his own and lived as much with him as with his brother.

No work of Seneca published before the death of Caligula has come down to us, but that his publications before that date were numerous and successful we know from a reference of Suetonius, who speaks of him as then at the height of his popularity—' tum maxime placentem.' His earlier books must have contained the bulk of the poetry dialogues and speeches mentioned by Quintilian.[2] Connected with the official class through his mother's family, witty, accomplished, original, and of gentle and conciliating manners, he appealed to the new generation by his daring innovations in manner and disregard for old conventions, by the freedom of his criticisms of the great orators and poets of the past, and by the singular power in which he was afterwards only excelled by Tacitus, of enshrining striking thoughts

[1] *Cons. ad Helv.* xvi.   [2] *Inst. Orat.* x. 1.

in short sentences that fixed themselves in the memory by their precision and completeness.

Caligula who, vain about everything, was especially vain of his oratorical powers, affected to despise the style of Seneca which he described in an oft-quoted phrase as 'sand without lime.' [1] The tyrant really possessed some genuine talent for invective—when angry his words came readily, he moved restlessly from place to place as he spoke, and his loud voice could be heard from a distance. He had also much skill in persuasion, and in his saner moments a winning manner that was almost irresistible.[2] It was his custom to make speeches before the Senate at the trials of great offenders, on which occasions the equestrian order was summoned by proclamation to attend the sittings, and the fate of the prisoner was often decided by the opportunities which an attack on the one hand or a defence on the other respectively offered to the imperial rhetoric.[3]

The ornamental manner of Seneca, studded with detached epigrams, contrasted strongly with the torrential eloquence of the emperor and on one occasion nearly cost him his life. He had spoken in the Senate in the emperor's presence with such eloquence and success that Caligula's jealousy was aroused, and the orator would have paid the extreme penalty for his triumph had not one of the imperial mistresses persuaded her lover that Seneca was in a rapid consumption and must

---

[1] 'Arenam sine calce' (Suet., *Cal.* 53).
[2] Josephus, *Ant.* xix. 2.   [3] Suet., *Cal.* 53.

shortly die in any case.[1]   It was doubtless to this
escape that he alluded when he wrote long afterwards to Lucilius that a disease, seemingly mortal
had prolonged the lives and proved the salva-
tion of many men.[2]   Whether from this alarm, or
from the state of his health, or because after the
death of his father he felt more at liberty to
follow his own inclinations, Seneca at this time
ceased to plead causes and devoted himself to
literature and philosophy.   Through his quaestorship he was a member of the Senate, where he
must have been present at the remarkable scenes
which followed the assassination of Caligula
and may have shared in the brief dream of a
restoration of their old supremacy from which
the senators were so rudely awakened by the
soldiers and the populace.

Scattered about in Seneca's works are stories
of the emperor whom he declared that Nature
could only have produced to show what the
greatest vices could effect when found in the
highest station; and they are interesting as the
only accounts of the tyrant, except that of Philo
Judaeus, which we have from an eye-witness.

Though one of the chief amusements of Caligula
was to hold up to ridicule the bodily imperfections
of others, his own appearance, Seneca tells us, in
his last years was itself well adapted to mockery.
He was bald, with stray hairs drawn down over
his forehead to conceal his baldness; his livid

[1] Dion, lix. 19.
[2] *Ep.* 78.   ' Multorum mortem distulit morbus ; et saluti illis
uit videri perire.'

complexion bore witness to the disorder of his mind ;
he had the wrinkled brow of an old woman, and
deep set under it wild and ferocious eyes. His
neck was hairy, his legs slender, and his feet
enormous.[1]

This description, overcharged perhaps at any
time, can only have been applicable to Caligula
as he was when the illness which destroyed his
mind had in its effects led him to those shameful
physical excesses and yet more shameful cruelties
and extravagances which degraded the last two
years of his principate. It cannot have been true
of the young Caius during the first months of his
reign, adored throughout the Empire, courteous,
generous, eloquent, and charming as he then
appeared while, with 'Youth on the prow and
Pleasure at the helm,' the ship of State rode
proudly along after the gloomy closing years of
Tiberius.

> Nothing [wrote Philo of that time] was to be seen
> throughout our cities but altars and sacrifices, priests
> clad in white and garlanded, the joyous ministers of the
> general mirth, festivals and assemblies, musical contests
> and horse-races, wakes by day and night, amusements,
> recreations, pleasures of every kind and addressed to
> every sense.

For the Roman aristocracy this halcyon period
came to an end with the recovery of Caius from
his illness,[2] for the exigencies of his luxury and
his megalomania having exhausted his treasury, a

---

[1] *De Constant. Sapientis*, 18. Cp. Suet., *Cal.* 50.
[2] With the people the emperor, like Nero, seems to have retained popularity to the end (Josephus, *Ant. Jud.* xix. i. 20, ii. 5).

veritable reign of terror began in order to supply
it from the spoils of rich victims, and increased
in intensity as the consciousness of guilt made
him suspect the designs of every man of note or
honesty. We are reminded of the death of Sir
Thomas More by Seneca's account of the serene
last hours of Julius Canus—one of the senators
who was put to death.

Canus Julius [he writes], a man of such commanding
greatness that his glory could not be obscured even
by the envy that always attaches to contemporaries,
was leaving the presence after a long altercation with
Caligula. ' I may as well tell you,' said the tyrant
by way of final rejoinder, ' so that you may not flatter
yourself with false hopes, that I have given orders for
your execution.' ' I thank you, most excellent prince,'
replied Canus. . . . He passed the ten days' interval
between sentence and execution with a mind free from
any kind of anxiety—indeed, the perfect tranquillity displayed in his words and actions almost passes belief.
He was playing at draughts when summoned by the
centurion in charge of the prisoners destined to die that
day. He counted his pieces, and said to the other player,
' Look, I have most left. Now you are not after my
death to pretend you have won.' And turning to the
centurion, ' I call you to witness,' he said, ' that I
am a piece to the good.' His friends were lamenting;
grieved at losing such a man. ' Why so sad ? ' he said.
' You will go on discussing whether the soul is immortal;
but I shall know in a few minutes.' His search for
truth persisted to the very end; and death itself afforded
him a new subject for investigation. He was accompanied by a philosopher and already stood near to the
altar on which the daily sacrifice was offered to our
god Caligula. What were the subjects of his thoughts ?
He declared his intention in that last rapid moment

carefully to observe whether the soul is conscious of its flight ; and he promised, if he discovered anything, to return and tell his friends where and what were the souls of the departed.[1]

It was impossible, as Seneca observed, to practise philosophy longer ; and this tranquillity in the midst of tempests argued a soul worthy of eternity.

To pity the fates of such men as Canus, Socrates, or Sir Thomas More would be to misunderstand them. But the emperor's freakish cruelty could not always be so thwarted ; and another incident related by Seneca is probably more characteristic of the time than that just recorded. There was a rich knight called Pastor whose son, having offended Caligula by the luxuriance of his hair and the elegance of his apparel, had been thrown into prison. Pastor came to the emperor to beg for his son's release; whereupon Caligula, as if suddenly reminded of something he had forgotten, ordered the youth to instant execution. The same day he invited the father to a banquet of one hundred covers ; and instructed a spy to observe his looks and conduct. Pastor came, showing no discomposure in his countenance. The feast was splendid, and the emperor drank to his health, plied him with wine, sent him ointments and garlands, treated him with especial courtesy, and bade him drown his cares in wine and good-fellowship. Pastor, a gouty old man, showed no sign of distress. He anointed himself with the oil, crowned himself with the garlands, and drank more than would have become him

[1] *De Tranquill. Animi,* c. 14.

had he been celebrating his son's birthday instead of his funeral. Why did he act thus when sick to death at heart ? He had another son.[1]

After Caligula, paying the penalty of his misdeeds, had died by the hand of a military tribune named Cassius Chaerea whom jeering personal insults had goaded into action, his uncle Claudius was discovered by a soldier hiding behind a curtain in a dark corner of the palace, dragged trembling from his hiding-place to the praetorian camp, and saluted as emperor by the soldiery.

On the news of the assassination the Senate met and resolved to restore the ancient constitution. They were at first supported by four urban cohorts ; and, for the last time in Roman history, the watchword was given by the consuls. Chaerea, who came to ask for it, was received with loud applause ; and the word chosen was *Libertas*. But the praetorian soldiers were determined that the supreme power should be their own gift ; and the people, far from desiring a return to the troublous times of the republic, regarded the emperor as a refuge against senatorial oppression and many masters as the worst of evils. On the second day only one hundred senators obeyed the summons of the consuls to the Temple of Jupiter, whence their own militia, after clamorously calling on them to choose an emperor, repaired, on their hesitation, to the camp and took the oath of fidelity to Claudius. The Senate thereupon submitted to necessity and decreed to Claudius all the honours attached to the principate.

[1] *De Ira*, ii. 33.

CHAPTER IV

THE new emperor had all his life been the object
of ridicule and contempt. He was fifty years
old, slow-minded, awkward in his motions, weak
on his legs, with tremulous head and hands
and a tongue too large for his mouth, fearful
to excess, apathetic to such a degree that no
insult could rouse in him resentment nor sufferings move him to pity, greedy and sensuous,
learned, pedantic, and absent-minded—honest
withal and well-meaning. As a child his mother
Antonia described him as a monstrosity, an
unfinished and abandoned attempt of Nature ;
and would say of a man that he was as great a
fool as her son Claudius. The Emperor Augustus,
noted for his grace and beauty, was ashamed
of his strange young kinsman ; and sequestered
him as much as possible from the public view.
He was kept in rough hands under the discipline
of pupilage for an unusually long time, and
admitted to no public honours until after the
death of Augustus, when Tiberius, who treated
him with more consideration, bestowed upon
him consular privileges while still denying him

the consulship. To this honour he was at last promoted by Caligula on his accession; but the mortifications he was compelled to endure at his nephew's Court exceeded all that he had previously experienced. He became the butt of the courtiers, and the victim of a thousand practical jokes played upon him to amuse the emperor. When he arrived late for dinner he was made to take the lowest place at the table; when he slept, as he usually did after satisfying his gluttonous appetite, they pelted him with olive stones or drew slippers over his hands, so that he might rub his eyes with them on waking. In Campania, however, where he had lived in retirement for many years on his exclusion from public business, in the intervals of the time given to the pleasures of the table and to the gaming which he loved, he had cultivated his understanding, and studied to some effect. He was an excellent Greek scholar, could make a good set speech when given time for preparation, and was the author of numerous works on historical and grammatical subjects.

Claudius began his reign well. He recalled the citizens unjustly exiled by his predecessor, and restored to them their goods; he repealed the oppressive new taxes; he administered justice personally with great assiduity, assisted by the consuls and praetors as assessors; he burnt all incriminating letters left by Caligula after having shown them to the persons concerned; he forbade the practice of making bequests to the emperor to which rich men

D

had been accustomed to resort as the only way of securing the disposition of the rest of their property in accordance with their will; and he restored to the cities from which they had been taken the statues which Caligula had brought to Rome. Other measures, such as the prohibition of Jewish ceremonies and the closing of public-houses, were of a more questionable character.

But the emperor's dull, timorous, and self-indulgent nature soon tired of well-doing; a creature of habit, and dreading change of any kind, he fell ever more completely under the influence of his dissolute, cruel, and rapacious wife Messalina, and of the freedmen to whose faces he was accustomed, until at last he became almost as neglected and despised as he had been before his accession. That no man is despised by others until he first despises himself, is an observation made by Seneca. Claudius despised himself and was comically conscious of his weakness. Once when a female witness was giving her evidence before the Senate, he said: ' This was my mother's maid and freedwoman; but she always regarded me as her master. I say this because there are still some people living in my house who do not regard me as their master.'

The empress and the freedmen, by working on his fears, were able to secure the condemnation of anyone whose estates they coveted or whose designs they suspected; and, by selling offices and justice, to amass huge fortunes for themselves. The two ruling passions of Claudius were for women and for the bloody spectacles of the arena. The first enslaved him to his successive wives and their favourites; the second made him find more satisfaction in the condemnations which provided material for his amusements than in the acquittal of accused persons.

Among those who were recalled from exile at the beginning of the new reign were the emperor's nieces, Julia and Agrippina, whom their brother Caligula, with his usual inconstancy, had banished after having heaped upon them every kind of honour. Julia was beautiful and ambitious; and Seneca, attached as he was to the house of Germanicus, was much in her society. The emperor also conversed with her often alone and seemed likely to fall under her influence. Messalina, who received from the proud beauty neither honour nor flattery, became jealous and alarmed. Julia's husband had been suggested as a possible successor to Caligula after his assassination,[1] and the remembrance of this may perhaps have enabled the empress to persuade Claudius again to banish her within a year of her recall from exile. However that may be, banished she was on a charge of adultery, and shortly afterwards put to death in her place of exile. Seneca, in the brief struggle for power between the empress and Julia, had attached himself to Julia, and shared her disgrace. He was accused of a criminal intrigue with Julia and banished to Corsica by a decree of the Senate.[2]

[1] Josephus, *Ant. Jud.* xix. 4.   [2] Dion Cassius, lx. 8.

A capital sentence was first proposed; but this, on the emperor's interposition, was changed to one of exile.[1]

From the barren and inhospitable shores of Corsica, where Seneca in middle life was detained for nearly eight years, he wrote, after an interval of six months from his arrival, the 'Consolation' to his mother Helvia which Bolingbroke has paraphrased in his 'Reflections upon Exile.' She must grieve, he tells her, neither for his sake nor her own. Not for his; for he is not unhappy. All that he has lost, all that fortune had so lavishly bestowed upon him—honours, money, fame—he had never held as if they were his own.

I kept a great interval between me and them. She took them, but she could not tear them from me. No man suffers by bad fortune, but he who has been deceived by good. If we grow fond of her gifts, fancy that they belong to us, and are perpetually to remain with us, if we lean on them, and expect to be considered for them, we shall sink into all the bitterness of grief as soon as these false and transitory benefits pass away, as soon as our vain and childish minds, unfraught with solid pleasures, become destitute even of those which are imaginary. But if we do not suffer ourselves to be transported by prosperity, neither shall we be reduced by adversity. Our souls will be of proof against the danger of both these states; and having explored our strength we shall be sure of it.[2]

All that is best in man, he urges, lies beyond

---

[1] *Consol. ad Pol.* xxxvii.: 'Deprecatus est pro me senatum, et vitam mihi non tantum dedit, sed etiam petiit.'

[2] *Consol. ad Helviam*, v. (Bolingbroke's translation.)

the power of others. It cannot be given ; it cannot be taken away. No change of place— and exile is nothing more—can take from him the glorious spectacle of the universe, nor the contemplating mind, roaming sacred and im- mortal through all the past and all the future, which is itself the noblest part of that universe. In support of his contention, not very con- vincing in itself, that since so many people quit their country of their own accord there can be no great hardship in an involuntary exile, Seneca gives an interesting account of the Rome of his day :

Consider Rome. How few of the inhabitants of that vast city are Romans ! They come from colonies and municipalities ; they flow together from the whole world. Some are brought by ambition ; some by their public duties ; others have been entrusted with missions ; luxury in search of opportunities, and industry seeking a larger field for action, entice others. Many come in search of pleasure ; many others to improve their minds by liberal studies ; while some bring their beauty and others their eloquence to market. Every race of man hastens to the city which offers the greatest prizes both to virtue and to vice.

If, then, his mother has no cause to grieve for him, neither should she grieve for herself. To the loss of a protector he knows that she is in- different, for she has never cared for the success of her sons in respect of her own interests. For her distress at her son's absence it is indeed harder to find a remedy. But he exhorts her to console herself with her other sons, to one of whom, Gallio, his honours will be chiefly valuable as ornaments to be laid at her feet ; to the other, Mela, his leisure, as it may enable him to enjoy more of her society. Her grandchild, Novatilla,[1] has recently lost her mother ; let Helvia be a mother to her and undertake the formation of her mind and manners ; she will find relief in an occupation so honourable. Her widowed sister, too, will prove to her the greatest comfort of all. It is not, however, to these that she must look for the real cure of her distress. That must be something beyond the reach of fortune ; and can only be found in the philosophical studies to which she must return. Philosophy, if in good faith she receive it within her soul, will leave no room for grief or for anxiety, or for the unprofitable troubles of a vain despair ; to all other faults and infirmities her breast has long been closed, with philosophy it will be closed to these also. Seneca ends his letter by describing his occupations on the island :

Since you will be constantly thinking of me whether you will or no ; since, indeed, I shall be with you more than your other children, not because I am dearer to you than they, but because the hand naturally seeks the painful spot, I will tell you how to think of me. Picture me, then, as happy and active, believe that all is as well with me as possible ; and all is really well when the soul, freed from cares, is at leisure for its own business, now taking pleasure in lighter studies, now in an eager pursuit of truth rising to the contem-

[1] This was the daughter of Gallio, then known as Novatus. To him Seneca dedicated his treatise *De Ira* published in 41, in the interval between the death of Caligula and his banishment to Corsica.

plation of its own nature and that of the universe. First, I consider the land and its situation ; next, the surrounding sea with its ebb and flow; then the space betwixt heaven and earth, and all its terror-striking and tumultuous appearances—the thunder and lightning, the clouds and hurricanes, the snow and hail ; and, lastly, my mind, leaving behind in its progress all that is below, pierces through to the heights, and enjoys the most beautiful spectacle of things divine, while, mindful of its eternity, it wanders through all that is past and dreams of all that through all the ages is to come.[1]

Another treatise, or fragment of a treatise, of a very different character has generally been ascribed to Seneca, and is supposed to have been written by him from his place of exile. This is the 'Consolation to Polybius' on the death of his brother. The rich freedman Polybius acted as literary secretary (*a studiis*) to Claudius—an important post under that learned prince—and was the author of prose translations of Homer into Latin and of Virgil into Greek. Not only is the 'Consolation' filled with the most abject flattery, both of him and yet more of the emperor, but it is flattery of such a kind, so maladroit, so obviously insincere, that it is hard to believe that it can ever have given pleasure to a human being ; and still harder to suppose that a learned, witty, and self-respecting man of the world, with the talent for pleasing which even his critics allowed Seneca to possess—a writer, moreover, very sensitive in the matter of his own reputation—could have imagined

[1] Peragratis humilioribus, ad summa prorumpit, et pulcherrimo divinorum spectaculo fruitur, aeternitatisque suae memor, in omne quod fuit futurumque est omnibus saeculis, vadit.

that it was capable of giving such pleasure. Claudius is complimented on the excellence of his memory—Claudius who inquired when Messalina was coming to dinner on the day after her execution [1]; Polybius is assured that he is on a level with Homer and Virgil, and that if he celebrates the acts of the emperor, in whose super-excellence he may find at once material for his history and a perfect model for historical composition, his work will be read by the latest posterity.

All the serious works of Seneca abound with lofty and striking thoughts so happily expressed that they stamp themselves upon the mind. Scarce any writer has been more often quoted with or without acknowledgment, or more deserves quotation, than he of whose treatises it has been said by one of the best of English critics that in their combination of high thought with deep feeling they have rarely, if ever, been surpassed. But high thought and deep feeling and moral dignity are alike absent from the 'Consolation to Polybius.' There is hardly a sentence in it worthy of quotation. The sentiment is commonplace where it is not affected. The writer observes

---

[1] *Consol. ad Pol.* xxxiii. : 'Tenacissima memoria retulit.' At first sight it seems incredible that Seneca could have written this except in conscious mockery, on which an unlimited faith in the emperor's dullness of apprehension could alone have emboldened him to venture. Even the flatterers of Louis XIV did not speak of his frugality or humility, nor would it have served them to do so. Flattery to gain its end must rest, however superficially, on some foundation of fact. But the learned Claudius may really have had a good verbal memory, often to be found in combination with the forgetfulness that comes from want of interest or attention

of the Stoic school to which Seneca belonged,
that its philosophers were more remarkable for
hardness than for judgment, and that had they
ever known what it was to suffer real adversity
they would have been compelled to recant their
doctrines and confess the truth. Moreover, Seneca
was no flatterer; for the noble panegyric of the
young Nero's clemency, written before the emperor
had forfeited all title to that virtue, and at a time
when it was of high importance to the commonwealth to interest the vanity which was his ruling
passion in the maintenance of his reputation in
that regard, was not flattery. Tacitus tells us that,
in Seneca's last message to Nero, he reminded
him that he was not given to adulation, adding
that no one knew this better than the emperor,
who had more reason to complain of his freedom
than of his servility.[1] Again, we are told that his
enemies, when plotting his fall, among many
other accusations charged him with aversion to
the emperor's favourite amusements, with depreciating his skill in horsemanship, and with thinking
scorn, and expressing it, even of the celebrated
voice.[2] He himself in the *De Clementia*, after
describing the golden age that had followed the
accession of Nero, says that he does not dwell
upon this picture to flatter the emperor's ears,
for that he would always rather trouble them by
a truth than please them by adulation. Dion

---

[1] Tac. *Ann.* xv. 61 : ' Nec sibi promptum in adulationes
ingenium. Idque nulli magis gnarum, quam Neroni, qui saepius
libertatem Senecae, quam servitium expertus esset.'
[2] *Ann.* xiv. 52.

Cassius, it is true, or his abbreviator, in the course of that singular invective against Seneca which contrasts so strangely with his earlier references to him, says that he addressed a book full of flattery from Corsica to the imperial freedmen; but adds, that on his return from exile he was ashamed of it and succeeded in suppressing it.[1] The conjecture of Diderot is, that the original treatise having perished that which we now possess is a forgery, composed by one of the numerous hostile critics of the life and writings of Seneca whom the conservative reaction against him in the second century called into existence, and that it was designed to load with odium and ridicule philosopher, freedman, and emperor alike. Much of it certainly reads like a parody; for those characteristics of Seneca, which are easy of imitation or caricature—the short sentences, the antitheses, the sudden turns, the rhetoric, and so forth—are all there; while there is little trace of his wit, or subtlety, or imagination, or depth, or mental elevation. The climax is replaced by anti-climax, the *sursum corda* by unworthy repinings of which Ovid might have been ashamed.

Yet glad though one might be to take refuge in the surmise of Diderot from a conclusion discreditable to Seneca, the internal evidence of his authorship is almost irresistible, and the circumstances in which a man of his temperament then found himself go far to explain, though they cannot altogether excuse, the temporary supersession of his finer instincts. There are passages

[1] Dion, lxi. 10.

in the treatise so characteristic of Seneca, both in manner and in matter, that they may seem to readers familiar with his other writings almost beyond the skill of an imitator.[1]

In the last chapter, after exhorting Polybius to distract his mind from his sorrow by plunging more deeply than ever into his learned studies, the writer, by a sudden and characteristic turn, admits that to root it out altogether would neither be possible nor even desirable.

Let your tears flow [he says] as nature will ; neither check nor encourage them. But do not hug your sorrow, or think that by so doing you honour the dead. Let your lost brother be often in your thoughts, talk naturally about him, meditate on his excellent qualities and describe them to others ; tell them all that he might have been had he lived. You will forget him and cease to honour his memory if you associate it with sadness, for the soul naturally turns away from what is painful.

These very arguments in the same sequence but in different words, this very advice and consolation, Seneca many years later addressed to another friend who had lost a little son.[2] The

___

[1] *E.g.* in chap. xxviii. : 'Si velis credere altius veritatem intuentibus, omnis vita supplicium est. In hoc profundum inquietumque projecti mare, alternis aestibus reciprocum, et modo allevans nos subitis incrementis, modo majoribus damnis deferens, assidueque jactans, nunquam stabili consistimus loco : pendemus et fluctuamur, et alter in alterum illidimur, et *aliquando naufragium facimus, semper timemus.*'

[2] *Ep.* 99. Cp. especially the reflection in the ' Consolation,' ' Naturale est enim, ut semper animus ab eo refugiat ad quod cum tristitia revertitur,' with that in the letter, ' Nemo enim libenter tristi conversatur, nedum tristitiae ' ; and the advice in the former, ' Omnia dicta ejus ac facta et aliis expone, et tibimet ipse commemora,' with that of the latter, ' De illo frequenter loquere, et memoriam ejus quantum potes celebra.'

coincidence may, of course, have its origin in the skill of a forger, but in that case he must have possessed a power of reserve very unusual in his kind ; for we have here no caricature, but an apparent example of the manner in which a train of thought recurs to a writer after a long interval of years when once again treating a similar subject.

Moreover, when we consider the circumstances in which Seneca then found himself, and the character of the man, we find it less difficult to believe in his authorship. In the prime of life, at the summit of his fame, ambition, and popularity (*'tum maxime placentem'*), having already entered through his quaestorship on the course of honours, married happily, and with a little son Marcus to whom he was tenderly attached, lately reunited to an adored mother whom he was not likely, if his exile were prolonged, ever again to see, he was suddenly thrown on a false charge into solitary exile in a barren and unhealthy island. And Seneca was not cast in an heroic mould. Though his gaze was on the stars, his feet were often in the mud. He himself humbly owned that he did not live up to his own ideals, and said with Horace, ' *Video meliora proboque, deteriora sequor.*' At the end of a few years of an exile which was destined to last for nearly eight, his spirit was broken. In the verses which he wrote in Corsica he speaks of himself as a corpse, and threatens a false friend—whoever that might be—now become his enemy, with the vengeance of the

dead.[1] Everything in the island displeased him
—the burning heat of the summer, the terrible
cold of the winter, the unfertile soil, the loneliness
and ruggedness of the country.[2]

The *cri de cœur* with which he ends the work
—perhaps the only sincere passage it contains—
bears strong witness to its authenticity :

I have strung together these thoughts [he writes
sadly] to the best of my ability (*utcunque potui*) from a
brain dulled and confused by the rust of a long inactivity.
They are, perhaps, quite unworthy of your attention,
quite unfitted for the object I had in view. But what
would you have ? How can a man overwhelmed by
his own misfortunes give comfort to others ? How can
he find the words he wants, or express his meaning
with felicity, when the only language he hears is one so
harsh and uncouth as to offend the ears even of the
more civilised among barbarians themselves ?

[1] Occisi jugulum quisquis scrutaris amici,
  Tu miserum necdum me satis esse putas ?
Desere confossum. Victori vulnus iniquo
  Mortiferum impressit mortua saepe manus.

[2] Non panis, non haustus aquae, non ultimus ignis :
  Hic sola haec duo sunt : exsul et exsilium.

CHAPTER V

A PALACE revolution at Rome in the year 48
brought the exile of Seneca to an end. Messalina,
made reckless by passion for her lover Silius,
resolved to risk all on a desperate throw, and,
at his urgent entreaty, agreed publicly to marry
him while Claudius was away at Ostia, after
which he was to seize the supreme power and
adopt her son Britannicus. The freedmen of
Claudius—Narcissus, Callistus, and Pallas—fearful
of losing their power and fortunes, hesitated
between three courses—either to do nothing, or
by secret threats of informing the emperor to
sever Messalina from Silius and force her to
abandon her designs, or without further delay
to communicate to Claudius what was going
forward and to risk the destruction that would
almost inevitably follow should Messalina once
more find an opportunity of controlling in
a personal interview the infirm will of the
timorous and besotted Caesar. The last course
recommended itself to Narcissus, at once the
boldest of the freedmen and the most attached
to the emperor. Claudius, informed, was on

his way back from Ostia, while in the garden of his palace the Bacchanalia were being celebrated with feasting and drinking and the wildest excesses. Messalina herself, as a Bacchante, her hair flowing and shaking the thyrsus, and Silius, crowned with ivy, led the revels ; and around them women, clad in skins, danced and sang in mad self-abandonment. One of the revellers, who had climbed to the top of a tree, was asked by his comrades what he saw : ' An awful storm coming up from Ostia,' he replied, in words afterwards regarded as a presage. Soon after came the news that Claudius knew all, and was returning post-haste to Rome and vengeance. The company scattered, and Messalina went out to meet the emperor with her children, Octavia and Britannicus. Narcissus, however, and his confederates contrived to prevent a meeting ; Claudius, stunned, stupid, and silent, left all to the freedman ; Silius was seized and put to death ; and the same night Messalina, by Narcissus' direction and the emperor's pretended order, suffered the same fate. The news was brought to Claudius at his dinner. He was not told whether she died by her own hand or by that of another, nor had he the curiosity to ask.

In the ensuing days [says Tacitus] he showed no signs of anger or of hatred, of joy or of grief, or of any human emotion ; nor was he moved in any degree by the sight either of his sorrowing children or of the triumphant satisfaction displayed by Messalina's accusers.[1]

[1] *Ann.* xi. 38.

The crisis over, the next object of the freedmen was to provide a successor to the place and
power of Messalina. The candidate of Narcissus
was Aelia Petina, a former wife of Claudius,
whom he had divorced for trivial reasons,[1] and
the mother of his daughter Antonia. Callistus
supported the claims of Lollia Paullina, a beautiful woman of immense wealth, who had
been married for a short time to Caligula.
Pallas espoused the cause of Agrippina, the
daughter of Germanicus, the sister of Caligula,
and the niece of the emperor. Claudius, the
slave of habit and easily governed by those
who had access to him, was exposed to the arts
of Agrippina, whose relationship gave her opportunities not enjoyed by her rivals of alluring
her amorous uncle. This relationship, however,
was in another way an obstacle to the alliance,
for Roman public opinion regarded such marriages
as incestuous, and Claudius himself had recently
been prevailed upon by Agrippina—who wished
to clear the way for her son's marriage—to cancel
the betrothal of his daughter Octavia to Lucius
Silanus by a false charge against that senator
of a criminal attachment to his sister. But the
courtier Vitellius, conspicuously servile even in
an age of servility, who had been employed to
concoct the charge against Silanus, again placed
his services at the disposal of Agrippina, and
easily persuaded the Senate to implore the
emperor, in the public interests, to contract this
marriage. At the same time such marriages

[1] ‘Ex levibus offensis’ (Suet., *Claudius*, 26).

were declared legal by a decree of the Senate. Claudius was married to Agrippina, her son Domitius was betrothed to Octavia and soon after adopted by the emperor under the name of Nero, Silanus slew himself, while Lollia, accused of consulting the Chaldaeans concerning the emperor's marriage, was driven into exile, and soon afterwards obliged to end her life by order of the empress.

But Agrippina [adds Tacitus], that she might not become known through evil deeds alone, obtained for Annaeus Seneca his recall from exile, and at the same time the praetorship. She thought that this would be a popular step, because of his high reputation for learning and eloquence, and she was, moreover, desirous to entrust to him the education of her son Nero, whose succession to the Empire he might be expected to further by his counsels, bound to Agrippina, as he would be, through gratitude, and hostile to the house of Claudius out of resentment of his exile.[1]

His return to Rome gave Seneca an opportunity of observing at close quarters the abuses of one of the worst governments that Rome had known. The chief feature of the reign of Claudius was the transfer of the administration from the ancient magistracies to a kind of imperial civil service, at the head of which were the freedmen of the imperial household. The provinces were governed for the most part by procurators, or direct representatives of the emperor, chosen not from among the senators, but from knights and freedmen ; and to these were committed, by

[1] *Ann.* xii. 8.

a decree of the Senate, the full judicial powers exercised in Rome by the emperor. In Rome Claudius became the minister of his freedmen secretaries, who accumulated vast fortunes by the sale of honours and commands, pardons and punishments, and at their pleasure rescinded the emperor's decisions, tampered with his warrants, and cancelled his donatives. Pallas, the most powerful of them, was his financial secretary, and the paramour of Agrippina. Those powers, we are told by Tacitus, for which in former times the rival orders of the State had so fiercely contended, which had passed from knights to Senate and from Senate to knights, and which had been the chief subject of the war between Marius and Sylla, were by Claudius given over to his nominees of any rank. The earlier Caesars had indeed given full powers to their representatives in provinces such as Egypt, specially reserved to them under the constitution of Augustus, but these had always been knights of distinction—it was reserved to Claudius to raise the authority of freedmen of his household to a level with his own and that of the laws.[1]

Claudius himself had a passion for sitting in judgment, which recalls the judge in Racine's comedy. In the early part of his reign he would sit all day in the Forum, or in the portico of one of the temples, hearing cases even on feast-days,

[1] Tac. *Ann.* xii. 60: ' Matios posthac et Vedios et cetera equitum praevalida nomina, referre nihil attinuerit; cum Claudius libertos, quos rei familiari praefecerat, sibique et legibus adaequaverit.' Also Suet., *Claudius*, 28.

and giving his decisions rather on what appeared to him general principles of equity than in obedience to the letter of the law. He had a loud, hoarse voice, difficult to follow, and though he sometimes showed sagacity on the bench, his judgments were, we are told, rash and unconsidered, and at times in the highest degree absurd. He would always decide against the absent in favour of the present, however involuntary such absence may have been, and in his anxiety to finish the greatest amount of business in the shortest possible time would often pronounce judgment after hearing only one side of the case. He made no attempt to preserve his dignity. Pleaders would pull him back to the bench by his cloak as he was hurrying off to his dinner. On one occasion a knight, accused of some offence by the meanest kind of witnesses, was so exasperated by the emperor's stupidity that he flung his papers at the imperial head.[1] So long, however, as Claudius tried cases openly no great harm was done. But after a time he was persuaded by his wives and freedmen to try political offenders *in camera*, with his unworthy favourites as assessors ; and the worst instances of cruelty and oppression that disgraced his reign were the result. The opinion of Seneca on these methods of administration may be gathered from the pasquinade on the apotheosis of Claudius which he afterwards wrote, and from the reforms in the early part of Nero's reign of which he was the author.

[1] Suet., *Claud.* xv.

Nero was twelve years old when adopted by
Claudius ; Britannicus, the emperor's son, three
years younger. They were now brothers in the
eye of the law, and Nero as the elder was given
precedence. Claudius announced the adoption in
a speech to the Senate, defending it on grounds
suggested to him by Pallas as a step taken in
the public interest with a view to the lightening
of his own labours and the provision of a support
for the childhood of Britannicus. He cited the
precedents of Augustus, who, in the lifetime of
his grandsons, had shared his power with his
stepsons, and of Tiberius, who had adopted his
nephew Germanicus and placed him on an equality
with his own son Drusus.[1]

In the year 51 Nero, then at the beginning of
his fourteenth year, assumed the *toga virilis*—a
ceremonial event of much importance in the life
of a young Roman of distinction, for it marked
the close of his childhood and his entrance into
public life. The usual time for this step was the
beginning of the fifteenth year, but Nero's powerful
protectors, anxious by his early advancement
to forward his succession to the principate,
anticipated by a year the natural period of his
majority. The Senate, with characteristic subservience, at once petitioned the emperor by
address that Nero might be empowered to enter
on the consulship in his twentieth year, that in
the meantime as consul designate he might be

---

[1] The contemporary genealogists observed that the adoption
of Nero was the first instance of an adoption into the Claudian
gens although the patrician family of the Claudii was one of
the oldest in Rome.

granted proconsular authority outside the city, and that the title of *princeps juventutis*, or prince of the youth, might be conferred upon him, to all which petitions Claudius was graciously pleased to assent. The soldiers and people were at the same time gratified with donatives.

Britannicus meanwhile was the object of general pity. He was thought a boy of much promise, though whether this opinion was well-founded, or whether it was merely the result of the interest naturally excited by his misfortunes, is a question left doubtful by the historian. He was neglected by the Court, deprived of the most faithful of his attendants, and surrounded by the creatures of Agrippina. At the circus games held in honour of Nero's majority the people marked the contrast between that prince's splendid attire adorned with the triumphal ornaments, and the humble *praetexta*, or boy's dress, of Britannicus, and the heir to the Empire seemed to be indicated by the distinction. The twelve-year-old child having continued to call his brother Domitius instead of Nero after the adoption, this was made matter of grave complaint by Agrippina to Claudius, who thereupon removed his former tutors and substituted for them the stepmother's nominees.

The most important step, however, taken by Agrippina in her son's interests was the reorganisation of the praetorian guard under a single chief. This force, to which the protection of the emperor's person was entrusted, was at that time under the joint command of Geta and Crispinus—two officers who owed their commissions to Messalina, and were believed to be devoted to the cause of her children. They were now removed, on the pretext that in the interests of discipline it would be better if the whole force were commanded by a single prefect, and Afranius Burrhus, a soldier of great distinction though of humble origin, was appointed in their room. History has little that is good to record of Agrippina, but it must be admitted to her credit that to her the world owed the rise to power of Burrhus and of Seneca, and so indirectly the five years of admirable government which those statesmen afterwards enabled it to enjoy.

Though Seneca obeyed the call of Agrippina to return to Rome and undertake the education of her son, he would have preferred to make other use of his recovered liberty. His own wish was to settle in Athens, as Atticus had done, and there to live a contemplative life in the study of moral and natural philosophy. He soon perceived how cruel and profligate was the disposition of his young pupil; and, though he persuaded himself that he had in some degree succeeded in mollifying it, he is said to have observed in conversation with his intimates that if ever the young lion tasted human blood the ingrained ferocity of his nature would assert itself.[1]

In the year 53 Nero, then in his seventeenth year, was married to Octavia ; and in the same year made his first appearance in the Senate as an orator by pleading the cause of the citizens of Ilium. This speech was in Greek. It dealt with

[1] Scholiast in Juv. *Sat.* 5, 109.

the legendary connection of Rome with Troy
and the descent of the Julian race from Aeneas ;
and won from the willing Senate, with the total
remission of taxes to the men of Ilium which was
its nominal, the applause which was its real, object.
This success was followed by a Latin speech
on behalf of Bonona which had been wasted by
fire, and a large subsidy in aid of the citizens
was the result. Of all the arts eloquence possessed the least attraction for Nero, and those
speeches, which excited great admiration, were
the compositions of Seneca.

   In the following year (54) a succession of strange
occurrences was thought to portend a revolution.
There were rumours of monstrous births ; tents
and standards were struck by lightning ; one
magistrate from each rank—a quaestor, an aedile,
a tribune, a praetor, and a consul—died within a
few months. The emperor's health was failing ;
and he was beginning to show some symptoms
of a returning affection for his son Britannicus,
whose interests were advanced by the still powerful
freedman, Narcissus. One day he exclaimed in
his cups that though he was fated to suffer the
crimes of all his wives, he was fated also to
punish them.[1] Agrippina, thoroughly alarmed,
resolved to act ; and with the help of a woman
called Locusta—a poisoner, we are told, long
considered a necessary instrument of the Court—
gave poison to her husband in his favourite dish
of mushrooms. The death was concealed, and

---

[1] Tac. *Ann.* xii. 64 : 'Fatale sibi, ut conjugum flagitia ferret,
dein puniret.'

Britannicus with his sister's kept within the palace, till all was in readiness for the peaceful succession of Nero. The Senate had been summoned on the news of the emperor's illness, and vows were offered for his recovery. At last at midday on October 13, the doors of the palace were flung open, Nero, escorted by Burrhus, presented to the guard and, no rival appearing, received with acclamation. Burrhus next brought him to the camp ; where, after he had addressed the soldiers and promised them a donative, he was saluted as *imperator*. The choice of the soldiers was confirmed by a decree of the Senate, and followed by the ready submission of the provinces.

CHAPTER VI

THE QUINQUENNIUM NERONIS, A.D. 54–59

THE first business of the Senate in the new reign was to decree a public funeral to Claudius, and his apotheosis. On the day of the funeral Nero made a speech composed for him by Seneca.[1] So long as he spoke of the antiquity, triumphs, and honours of the Claudian race, of the unbroken prosperity in external affairs that distinguished the reign of Claudius, and of the taste of that prince for letters and the arts, he was heard with approval; but when he went on to praise the late emperor's wisdom and foresight his hearers could not restrain their laughter; 'though the speech,' adds Tacitus with characteristic ambiguity, 'like all Seneca's compositions, was of remarkable elegance and charm, for indeed there was something in the man's turn of mind which was exactly fitted to the taste of that generation.' It is probable that the failure of this part of his speech did not greatly displease the imperial orator; for in spite of the magnificence of the funeral ceremonies, the memory of Claudius and the apotheosis itself

---

[1] It was observed that he was the first of the emperors whose speeches were written for him by others.

were the subjects of contemptuous ridicule at the Court. Claudius, said Gallio, in allusion to the hooks with which the bodies of condemned criminals were drawn down the steps of the Gemoniae and flung into the Tiber, had been dragged to heaven with a hook.[1]   Nero exclaimed that now it was clear that mushrooms were food for the gods ; and Seneca produced his famous *jeu d'esprit* under the title of the ' Apocolocyntosis or Pumpkinification of Claudius.'

In this satirical medley of prose and verse the arrival of Claudius at the gate of heaven with dragging foot and perpetually shaking head is described ; his reception by Hercules, who, accustomed as he is to monsters, is so perturbed by the sight of this one that he has to look closely before he can distinguish ' a sort of man,' and believes himself at odds with a thirteenth labour ; the delight of Claudius on hearing himself addressed in Greek, and the hope he derives therefrom of being able to add his own histories to the library of heaven ; the debate in heaven on his admission, and his expulsion at the instance of Augustus, who makes his maiden speech on the occasion. Next we hear of his descent to the infernal regions, under the escort of Mercury, by way of Rome, where the sight of his own funeral taking place amid general rejoicings makes him understand for the first time that he is dead ; of his delight on his arrival in hell to find himself in the midst of old friends, and his discomfiture at the unexpected reply to his inquiry by what good fortune

[1] Dion, lx. 35.

they all came to be there assembled—' You sent
us, murderer of all your kin '; of his trial, followed
by the condemnation to play at dice for ever with
a bottomless box ; and, finally, of his conveyance
to Caligula, who claimed him as his slave on the
plea of having often been seen beating him on
earth, and his eventual assignment as a clerk
to Menander, Caligula's freedman.   The piece,
witty and amusing though it be and unique of
its kind in Latin literature, shows a lack of
good feeling more characteristic of the time
than of Seneca, to whose reputation it can add
nothing.

The idleness, dissipation, and hatred of business
which distinguished the young emperor combined
with his vanity and love of popularity to throw
the whole administration of affairs in the early
part of his reign into the hands of Seneca and
Burrhus.   The single object of these two statesmen appears to have been the public good, and as a
consequence of this singleness of aim no shadow
of misunderstanding from first to last marred the
harmony of their mutual relations—a rare circumstance, as Tacitus remarks, in the history of public
men.   The virtues of the one supplemented
those of the other.   Burrhus was known for the
austerity of his life, the bluntness of his speech,
and the severity of his military discipline ; Seneca,
notwithstanding his stoicism, was a courtier and a
wit, he knew how to charm others without loss of
personal dignity, and was a master of eloquence.

After the funeral ceremonies of Claudius had
been completed and the pretence of mourning

laid aside,[1] Nero made his entry into the Senate-
house and announced the policy of the new reign
in a speech composed for him by Seneca. After
reminding his hearers that his boyhood had been
passed in no scenes of civil or domestic discord,
and that he had consequently no injuries to avenge
or hatreds to satisfy, he proceeded to touch on
the abuses of the late régime and to explain the
new system of government which he proposed to
follow. The reign of law, he said in effect, was
to replace that of caprice. He did not propose to
busy himself personally in the trial of offenders ;
the scandal of the secret investigations in the
Cabinet where accusers and accused alone were
present was to end ; the court was no longer to be
a market where offices, privileges, and pardons
were sold to favourites ; his private fortune must
be distinguished from the public revenue, his
household from the ministers of the republic.
The Senate were to be reinstated in its ancient
functions, and consular tribunals to be restored
to Italy and the senatorial provinces, with the
right of appeal to the Senate.[2] Let the Senate,
he said in conclusion, address themselves to the
administration of the republic ; he himself would
take thought for the armies committed to his care.

This speech was heard with exultation by

[1] ' Peractis tristitiae imitamentis ' (*Ann.* xiii. 4).

[2] This refers to the division of the provinces into imperial
and senatorial provinces made by Augustus—the latter being
administered by the Senate, the former directly by himself
through procurators. Under Claudius the distinction had been
practically abolished, and the whole Empire, with a few excep-
tions, such as Achaia, governed by the emperor's procurators
who, like Felix in Judaea, were often freedmen.

the senators. They decreed that it should be engraved in letters of silver, and read publicly at the beginning of each new year, hoping to bind the emperor by this recurring publication to observe the charter of liberties it contained.[1] Nor were those hopes at first deceived. The Senate, under the direction doubtless of Seneca and Burrhus, made early use of its recovered liberties, and Acts were passed dealing with recent abuses. The young emperor himself declared his intention of walking in the steps of his ancestor Augustus, and seized every opportunity of showing courtesy, humanity, and liberality. The heavier taxes were reduced or repealed. Informers were discouraged, and their fees reduced to a fourth. The ruinous burdens which successful candidates for honours had been compelled to endure were reduced within more reasonable limits ; appeals were instituted from the judges to the Senate ; the law against forgery was strengthened ; and lawyers' fees were regulated.[2]

These reforms were opposed by Agrippina, who had no wish for the downfall of a system by which she had profited so largely. But her influence was already on the wane. When her power had been threatened in the preceding reign, she had contrived the death of Claudius in order to preserve it, but she was now to find that her ambition had overleapt itself. At first, indeed, all had gone well. Her violence and imperious temper intimidated Nero and bent him to her wishes, though he longed to shake off a detested

<hr>

[1] Dion Cassius, lxi. 3.   [2] Suet. *Nero*, x.

yoke. He began by heaping honours on the mother to whom he owed the Empire. She accepted these honours as her due, and was imprudent enough continually to remind him of his obligations. The assassination of Silanus, Proconsul of Asia, gave early proof of what might be expected from the continuance of her power. Silanus had owed his safety in the preceding reigns to his inactivity and notorious lack of ambition, but as a descendant of Augustus he had been spoken of as a possible rival to Nero, and he was the brother of another Silanus for whose death under Claudius Agrippina had been responsible. Agrippina, therefore, caused him to be poisoned at his own table, employing as her agents two men charged with the management of the imperial estate in the province. The crime was committed with so little attempt at concealment that it was a secret to none. Narcissus, too, who had opposed her marriage with Claudius, was imprisoned with such severity that he took refuge in self-destruction. Other executions would have followed but for the interposition of Seneca and Burrhus. Nero, who was innocent of the murder of Silanus and had been opposed to the punishment of Narcissus, was glad to support his two ministers, and in so doing to satisfy his vanity by earning a reputation for clemency and good government. Moreover, the man who had most influence with Agrippina was the fabulously rich freedman Pallas, her paramour, whose moroseness and arrogance had made him universally detested. The destruction of the power of the freedmen was a preliminary

step essential to the restoration of the just and
humane administration contemplated by Seneca,
and so long as Agrippina remained all-powerful
that object could not be effected.

An incident that occurred before Nero had
been many months emperor served to show
which side had gained the victory in this brief
struggle for power between the reformers and
the upholders of the old system. Agrippina
had been accustomed during the principate of
Claudius to appear in the company of that feeble
sovereign on state occasions and openly to share
his sovereignty. Nor had she anticipated that
her position in that respect would be changed for
the worse by the succession of her son to power.
But one day Nero was seated on his throne and
about to receive some Armenian ambassadors,
when his mother entered the audience chamber
and advanced with the intention of seating herself
beside him to share in their reception. Though
all who were present were indignantly conscious
that such an assessor would lower the imperial
dignity in the eyes of the Armenians, Seneca
alone had the courage to intervene. At his
whispered suggestion the prince left his throne
and advanced down the hall, as if out of respect
to greet his mother. An excuse was then found
for postponing the reception of the delegates, and
the scandal was averted.

Seneca has been charged with ingratitude to
Agrippina, to whom he owed his return from
exile and the appointment as Nero's tutor on
which were founded his wealth and greatness.

But he had to choose between resistance to the power of the empress and the abandonment of his projects of reform, and it is by no means clear that he ought to have chosen the latter. In his treatise *De Beneficiis* he says that if a man has received favours from a tyrant he ought to repay him with what benefits he can, so long as he can do so without injury to others.[1] To have supported the cruel and corrupt influence of Agrippina would have been signally to have violated this condition ; while if he had retired from public life, deserted Burrhus, and surrendered his opportunities of serving the State, he would none the less have been accused of ingratitude by Agrippina, who had counted on his active support.

At all events the prosperity of the first five years of the reign of Nero, the famous *quin-quennium Neronis*, during which the emperor, abandoning himself to his pleasures, left the whole business of the State to Seneca and Burrhus, silenced for the time the detractors of those statesmen. The Emperor Trajan was afterwards wont to declare that this, in his judgment, was the period in which the Romans enjoyed the best government under the Empire.[2] Even the malicious historian Dion Cassius, enemy though he was to Seneca's reputation, writes that these statesmen, once the full control of affairs had fallen into their hands, exercised it with a justice

[1] *De Benef.* vii. 20.
[2] ' Merito Trajanus saepius testatur procul differre cunctos principes Neronis quinquennio ' (Aurelius Victor, *de Caesar.* c. 5).

and an ability which won for them universal
applause.[1]   It was something when in the strange
course of human destiny supreme power over the
civilised world had fallen into the hands of a
vicious and worthless youth, not only to have
saved five years from the wreck, but even to have
made them memorable for their excellence.   That
this feat was accomplished by Seneca cannot
be denied, though the means he employed to retain and confirm his power unquestionably need
defence.

The steps taken at the end of the year (54)
to repel a Parthian invasion of Armenia, and
the appointment of Corbulo, an able general,
whose sole claim to promotion lay in his merits
to the chief military command there, increased
the confidence felt in the administration, and
were taken as signs that the era of appointments
by favour and intrigue was at an end.   The
Senate wished to erect gold and silver statues to
the emperor, and to call the month of December
by his name, but he modestly declined these
honours.   Nor would he listen to delators who
brought accusations of disaffection against knights
and senators.

The year 55, the second of the reign, was
marked by fresh acts of a wise indulgence to
which the Romans had been unaccustomed since
the early years of Tiberius.   The young emperor
pledged himself to a policy of conciliation in
numerous speeches in which the world recognised
the hand of Seneca.   These speeches, adds Tacitus,

[1] Dion, lxi. 4.

F

he put into the prince's mouth either in order to display his own talents or else that all might know in what honourable principles he had trained the mind of his imperial pupil. Most of the historian's references to Seneca are marked by a certain reserve or unfriendly suggestion as of one anxious not to be unfair yet resolved to do no more than bare justice to a man with whom he was out of sympathy. In this instance it would seem, on the face of it, at least as probable that in interesting Nero's vanity in a reputation for clemency, and engaging him by public professions to maintain it, Seneca was acting on public grounds as that he was merely endeavouring to win applause for himself.

It was at this time that he addressed to the emperor the finely conceived and nobly expressed treatise *De Clementia*, the first part of which has been happily preserved to us. In this treatise the philosopher described the emperor as not only the principle of unity that linked together the vast regions of the Empire, but also the mind that directed the huge body, the limbs of which it restrained from mutual destruction. The republic, he said, and Caesar have so grown together that they cannot be torn asunder without the destruction of both, and the union is such that Caesar will practise clemency to his subjects for the same reason that a man is merciful to his own members. Bleeding or a surgical operation may be required, but he will shed no blood nor inflict any pain that is not inevitably necessary for the common good. Seneca pictures the young

prince serenely contemplating the vast masses
of his subjects—so various in race and character,
so ready for internecine strife, kept in peace only
by their common allegiance ; and thus speaking to
himself :

From out the host of mortal beings I have been
chosen and thought worthy to do the work of the gods
upon the earth. I have been given the power of life
and death over all the nations. To determine the
condition and to control the destinies of every race
and of every individual is my absolute prerogative.
Whatever Fortune has to give, through my work she
gives it ; from my replies as from a fountain peoples
and cities draw their happiness. There is no prosperity
in all the world save by my favour and allowance. These
countless swords, sheathed by my peace, at a sign from
me would leap from their scabbards. It is in my power,
were I so minded, utterly to destroy or expatriate whole
nations ; their liberties are mine to give or to withhold ;
kings at my word become slaves ; the brow of whom I
will I encircle with a diadem ; cities come into being or
are lost according to my will. In this supreme position
neither anger, nor the natural impetuosity of youth,
nor the foolish stubbornness of men hardly to be borne
by the most patient of tempers, nor even that dire
ambition so common in princes drawing them on to
display their power by terror-striking acts, have ever
moved me to inflict a single unjust punishment. The
humblest blood is precious to me ; my sword lies buried
in its sheath ; if a suppliant has nothing else to plead,
yet as a man he will find favour in my sight. My severity
I keep concealed ; my clemency in the open and ready
for use. I have rescued the laws from the obscurity
and neglect into which they had fallen, and I observe
them as if I too had to render an account of my actions.
I have been touched by the youth of one prisoner, by the
age of another ; the rank of some, the helplessness of

others, have moved me to pardon ; where no other reason for mercy could be found, I have forgiven for the pleasure of forgiving. If this day the immortal gods were to bid me give an account of my stewardship of the human race the reckoning would show no loss. ' It is true, Caesar,' replies Seneca ; ' and you may claim with confidence that of all the citizens entrusted to your care not one either through open violence or secret treachery has been lost to the commonwealth. Your only ambition has been to be praised for the rarest quality of all—a glory vouchsafed to none of your predecessors—the glory of innocence. You have not wasted your pains. That singular goodness of yours has not been valued grudgingly or unwillingly. Your subjects are grateful indeed. No individual was ever so dear to another as you, their great and lasting treasure, are to the whole Roman people. But you have undertaken a heavy task. In this first year you have given us a taste of your rule, and have set up a new standard by which you yourself will be judged. No one will any longer care to remember the times of the divine Augustus or the early years of Tiberius ; you yourself have supplied the only model by which men will wish that you yourself should be guided.'

No man, wrote Seneca, in one of his letters, can paint a picture though his colours are all ready unless he knows exactly what it is he wishes to paint. In this picture of the innocent autocrat who, making his choice between the two great rival forces by which men are governed, finds his strength in their love rather than in their fear, Seneca anticipated, as he often does, the teaching of Christianity. There may be flattery in his words, but it is flattery of a noble sort and directed to a noble end. So far Nero, guided by his ministers, had really governed his subjects with justice and humanity ; and would have almost deserved the praise he received had not this result been attributable rather to his aversion from business and love of popularity than to any worthier motive.

In this second year of his reign Nero, who from the first had abhorred his guiltless and unhappy wife Octavia, fell passionately in love with a young freedwoman named Acte.   The affair was confided to the prince's boon companions— chief among whom was Otho, afterwards emperor —and to the ministers, but was otherwise a secret. Seneca and Burrhus, hopeless of reconciling Nero to Octavia, regarded without displeasure his in- fatuation for a good-natured girl, whose influence injured no one while it satisfied the dangerous passions of her lover in a manner harmless to the commonwealth.   But Seneca carried his com- plaisance too far if it was at his suggestion that his most intimate friend, Annaeus Serenus, captain of Nero's bodyguard, to disguise the real intrigue, played the part of Acte's lover and openly sent her the presents which really came from the emperor.   This artifice at first deceived Agrippina ; but she soon came to know the truth.   Always in extremes, she stormed, menaced, and insulted ; and then, finding her rage of no effect, passed to the most abject flattery and submission with no better success.   Nero, when the discovery was first made, endeavoured to conciliate her by a rich present of robes and jewellery ; but this she received with disdain, exclaiming that she had given him all and he was returning her a part.

Her subsequent submission merely emboldened him to dismiss her minion Pallas from all his offices, and openly to bring her power to an end.

On this Agrippina, flinging prudence to the winds, gave a free rein to the ungovernable temper which she had inherited from her mother. Britannicus, she exclaimed, was now of an age to succeed to that inheritance which her own injustice had transferred to a usurper. Since so many crimes had been committed in vain she would confess them all, and, since by the mercy of the gods Britannicus still lived, make reparation. She would go to the camp accompanied by Britannicus and present herself to the soldiers— bidding them choose between the pedant Seneca, who with the low-born cripple Burrhus had the audacity to aspire to govern the world, and the daughter of Germanicus.[1] She was to find, however, that an emperor was easier to make than to unmake.

To the unfortunate Britannicus her support proved even more disastrous than her hostility. Nero's latent jealousy and suspicion had already been roused to activity by an incident which had occurred during the Saturnalia of the preceding December. There was a game played by Roman boys consisting in the choice of a ' king ' by lot, whose commands, whatever they might be, the rest were obliged one by one to obey. On this occasion the lot fell on Nero, and to expose Britannicus to ridicule he ordered him to stand in the middle and sing a song. The boy obeyed;

[1] Tac. *Ann*. xiii. 14.

and sang in so pathetic a manner the misfortunes of one who had been driven from his father's house and despoiled of his inheritance, that he moved all his hearers to compassion.

Agrippina was doubtless aware of her son's suspicions when she threatened him with the rivalry of Britannicus; but she does not seem to have anticipated their natural result in that prince's destruction. Such, however, it proved. The ministrations of Locusta—the recognised Court poisoner—were again employed; and Britannicus was poisoned at a banquet in the presence of Nero and his Court. The wine, tried by his taster, was designedly so heated that he called for water to cool it, and in the water thus added to his drink a deadly poison was administered. So rapid was its effect that he fell back instantly deprived of sense. A thrill of horror ran through the company. The more imprudent dispersed; others better advised remained seated and looked fixedly at Nero for their cue. He with an air of indifference remarked that Britannicus had from his infancy been subject to such fits and that he would soon be better. There was a short silence, and then the feast proceeded as if nothing had happened. The terror and consternation visible in the countenance of Agrippina served to convince all present that she was as innocent of complicity in the murder as Octavia herself, who in spite of her extreme youth had been taught by adversity to conceal every symptom of feeling. In the same night the ashes of Britannicus were hurriedly buried in the

Campus Martius—all preparations having been made beforehand. In a subsequent edict Nero defended these hasty obsequies and the omission of the usual funeral speeches and ceremonies by a reference to ancient usage ; and, bewailing the loss of his brother's support, expressed his reliance, as the last of a family born to Empire, on the enhanced devotion of Senate and people. The estate of Britannicus, his houses, and villas, were divided by the emperor among the gravest and most honoured of his own friends, with the object, it was thought, of binding them to acquiescence. It would not have been safe to refuse the imperial gifts, but the conduct of such men as Seneca and Burrhus in accepting them did not escape animadversion.[1]

No presents, however, could soften the anger of Agrippina. Her friends were admitted to secret interviews ; she raised money from every quarter ; she caressed Octavia ; she made court to the soldiers ; and extolled the qualities of certain of the chief among the nobility as though she were seeking a leader for her party. When the news of these proceedings reached Nero he retaliated by discharging her bodyguard and removing her from the palace to another house, where, always accompanied by a large body of centurions, he made her a few brief and formal visits.

Agrippina's enemies now thought that their

---

[1] Tac. *Ann.* xiii. 18 : 'Nec defuere, qui arguerent viros gravitatem asseverantes, quod domos, villas, id temporis, quasi praedam divisissent.'

time had come.   Junia Silana, formerly her intimate friend and her rival in race, in beauty, and in
wantonness, but whose friendship had been turned
by a private quarrel into hatred, devised a plot
for her ruin.   Two clients of Silana, Iturius and
Calvisius, agreed to accuse the empress-mother of
a plot to overthrow Nero and to marry Rubellius
Plautus, a descendant through his mother of
Augustus, whom she would at the same time
place on the throne.   An actorc alled Paris, a
favourite minister of Nero's pleasures, was chosen
to reveal the pretended conspiracy.

Late one night, when the emperor was heavy
with wine, Paris entered his apartment with
tragic countenance and told his story.   The
first impulse of the terrified Nero was to give
order for the immediate execution of his mother
and Plautus, but he was dissuaded from doing
so by Burrhus and Seneca, who pointed out the
flimsy nature of the evidence against Agrippina
and the injustice of condemning her unheard.
The next morning Seneca and Burrhus proceeded to her house to inquire into the matter,
when she defended herself with spirit and success,
and demanded an audience of her son.   This
was granted ;   and completed the discomfiture
of her opponents.   Agrippina knew her son
well.   Disdaining to defend herself or to remind
him of his obligations, she boldly denounced
her accusers and demanded redress.   Nero, who
was as cowardly as he was cruel and treacherous,
feared those who defied him, and was accustomed to submit to his imperious mother.   He

promised all she asked. Silana was exiled for life ; Calvisius and Iturius for a term of years. Paris could not be spared and was forgiven. On this occasion, at least, Seneca and Burrhus rescued their former patroness from urgent danger.

CHAPTER VII

SENECA IN POWER

THE two following years (56 and 57) were quiet and uneventful. Peace reigned throughout the Empire, while in Rome the Senate, to which a part of its former authority had been restored, was occupied in legislative work, especially in connection with the administration of the revenue, which was transferred from the quaestors, to whom it had been entrusted by Claudius, to prefects who had served as praetors, and were men of longer experience. The decaying colonies of Capua and Nuceria were assisted by the introduction of new drafts of veterans and by subsidies. The Roman import duty on slaves was remitted ; but this, observes Tacitus, was found to be a boon rather in appearance than in reality to the importer, since he had already succeeded in transferring the tax to the consumer by adding it to his price.[1]

The provincial cities in Italy and elsewhere in the Empire enjoyed at this time an almost complete system of self-government. Their

---

[1] *Ann.* xiii. 31 : ' Quia, cum venditor pendere juberetur, in partem pretii emptoribus accrescebat.'

institutions had been modelled on those of republican Rome, and unlike those of Rome had endured in reality as well as in name. Of municipal magistrates the duumviri, answering to the consuls, presided over the municipal senate and exercised judicial powers ; the aediles were in charge of works and buildings and of the police ; while the quaestors administered the revenue. These magistrates were all elected by the people,[1] and were expected by public opinion to show their sense of the honour conferred upon them by a gift to their city. Aqueducts, roads, temples, theatres were habitually presented to their fellow-citizens by magistrates during their term of office. Thus the labour of the community was directed to public and not to private uses by those to whom the possession of money had given the power of choosing its direction, and great prosperity was the result. ' The whole world is full,' wrote the rhetorician Aristides under the Antonines, ' of gymnasia, fountains, porticoes, temples, workshops, and schools . . . all the towns are radiant with elegance and splendour, and the land has become one vast garden.'

In Rome itself all was not so well. The administration was, it is true, well conducted by Seneca and Burrhus, to whom the emperor left the whole business of government. But the detestable character of the degenerate aesthete on the throne began so early as the year 56 to make itself felt. The public atrocities which followed

---

[1] The suffrage was universal and the elections by ballot.

his personal assumption of the government were foreshadowed by the crimes and extravagances by which his private life was already stained. His favourite nocturnal amusement at this time was to sally forth disguised from his palace into the streets, accompanied by his boon companions, whom he would cause to attack those whom they met, insult women, break open doors, and plunder shops. Sometimes the people attacked, not recognising their assailant, would defend themselves vigorously ; and the marks of their fists would be visible on the emperor's face the next day; so, to avoid such accidents for the future, he directed a body of gladiators to follow him at a distance, and to use their weapons if matters became serious. When it became known that Caesar was the hero of these nocturnal expeditions his example was followed by others, whose objects were more practical, and who used his name to secure their booty; until, according to the historian, Rome at night came to resemble a captured city given over to plunder. His encouragement of faction fights in the theatres was scarcely less mischievous.

These years marked the high tide of Seneca's prosperity. ' Seneca,' wrote the elder Pliny of that time, ' than whom no man was ever less beguiled by appearances, was then the prince of learning and at the summit of that power by which he was afterwards overwhelmed.' [1] The

---

[1] Pliny, *N.H.* xiv. 4 : ' Novissime Annaeo Seneca, principe tum eruditionis ac potentiae quae postremo nimia fuit super ipsum, minime utique miratore inanium.'

most powerful statesman was at the same time the most admired writer of the day. His speeches, treatises, and poetry were in everybody's hands. The rising generation, says Quintilian, would scarcely read any other author,[1] and the concoction of epigrams and aphorisms (*sententiae*) after his manner became the literary fashion.

His nephew Lucan, son of the prudent Mela, was the most brilliant of the poets of the new school. After other more conventional essays in poetry he published, while still under twenty-five years of age, the first part of an epic poem on the civil wars, written on a completely new plan. Boldly discarding the whole of the supernatural machinery of Olympus, considered ever since the days of Homer an indispensable adjunct to an epic, he described events and characters with what historical accuracy his researches could supply. He had no respect for remote antiquity— '*famosa vetustas miratrixque sui*'[2]—the stirring scenes of the century which preceded his own offered material enough for his rushing, impetuous rhetoric. Why blunt its force and lose all the interest attaching to the connection between character and events by invoking the interposition of shadowy beings in whom his readers had ceased to believe? Keenly interested in the world as it appeared to him amid the strife of men, and a violent partisan, he was, like Byron, of too passionate a nature, and lived too much in the present to find time for subjective musings,

---

[1] Quint. x. i : ' Tum autem solus hic fere in manibus adolescentium fuit.'   [2] *Phars.* iv. 654–5.

for the wonder and pathos of Virgil, or the wide
surmise of Lucretius. He had, as Quintilian observed, the temperament rather of an orator than
of a poet.[1] The romance of reality, the picture
of a rudderless world and of the interaction of
events and character, for the first time challenged
the ruling idea of every previous epic—the idea
that men were but irresponsible puppets moved
by divine agencies which the seer's eyes were
alone strong enough to detect. The Senecas were
a daring race of innovators who held Olympus in
scanty respect.

I am not such a fool [wrote Seneca in one of his
letters] as to repeat the old soothing lullabies of Epicurus,
and to tell you that the fear of hell is vain, that no Ixion
is bound to a revolving wheel, that the shoulder of
Sisyphus rolls no stone up the hill, that no entrails
can be devoured and restored every day. No one is
childish enough to fear Cerberus and the darkness and the
ghostly appearance of spirits clinging to their skeletons.
Death either consumes us or frees us. If we escape,
better things await us when we have laid down our
burden ; if we are consumed, nothing remains.[2]

Lucan, in the course of the extravagant compliment to Nero which disfigures the first book
of the ' Pharsalia,' declares that the worship of
all the other gods has been rendered superfluous
at Rome by the presence of that amiable prince ;
and entreats him, when he takes his final leave
of earth, to take up his position well in the centre

---

[1] *Inst. Orat.* **x.** **1.** 90: 'Lucanus ardens et concitatus et
sententiis clarissimus et, ut dicam quod sentio, magis oratoribus
quam poetis imitandus.'
[2] *Ep.* 24.

of heaven lest the balance of the universe should be imperilled. In the later and republican part of the poem he contrasts in a famous line the triumphant injustice of the gods with the defeated virtue of Cato.[1] And we know that Gallio cared for none of these things.

Nero was himself a poet as well as a painter, a sculptor, a musician, and a singer. His first step on acceding to the principate was to summon to the palace Terpnus, the most celebrated lute-player of the day, in whose company he would spend half the day and half the night listening to his performances and receiving his instructions. Lucan, too, the nephew of the chief minister, was at first in high favour. Nero recalled him from Athens, where he was finishing his education, admitted him to the company of his intimate friends, and made him quaestor. But Lucan's poetic success afterwards excited the emperor's jealousy; who probably also disapproved of his disregard for the traditional rules of composition. The first publication of poems in Rome consisted in their recitation by the author to an invited company of friends.[2] One day when Nero was present at a recitation by Lucan of a newly composed poem he affected to be weary, and suddenly left the room without waiting for the end. This was an insult the sensitive poet could not forgive. He revenged himself by lampoons and epigrams directed against the emperor and his friends, who

---

[1] i. 128: 'Victrix causa deis placuit, sed victa Catoni.'

[2] Attendance on such occasions was an imperative social obligation, which became to many a nuisance almost intolerable.

retaliated by forbidding him either to recite or
to publish any further poems. Nothing could
have been thought of more calculated to mortify
and enrage a young author intoxicated by his
popularity and his public and private triumphs.
It was then that he wrote the last part of the
'Pharsalia,' with its stinging attacks on the
imperial system and its exaltation of the heroes
of the republic.

One result of the quarrel between Nero and
Lucan was the attack directed on the new school
by writers connected with the Court. Conspicuous
among these was Petronius, the leader of Nero's
dissolute friends, the arbiter of fashion, an artist
in luxury, a man for whose judgment in such
matters the emperor had so high a respect that
he thought no diversion agreeable or refined until
Petronius had stamped it with the hall-mark of
his approval. In a kind of picaresque character-
novel, unique of its kind in surviving Latin literature, Petronius introduced an old poet called
Eumolpus, very much out-at-elbows, to plead the
cause of classical tradition against new methods.
Eumolpus complains that in these degenerate
times, when a man has learnt the art of making
glittering epigrams in the schools of rhetoric
and proved a failure at the Bar, he turns to the
composition of poetry as to a haven of rest and
enjoyment. Yet really to be a poet he should be
steeped in literature, he must avoid all popular
or hackneyed diction, his epigrams must not
stand out abrupt and disconnected from the
body of his discourse, but be woven with

concealed art into the texture of the material they adorn. Homer and Virgil, and Horace with his exquisite felicity—*curiosa felicitas*—prove this.

For instance [he adds, in direct allusion to the 'Pharsalia'], a man who should be daring enough to undertake to sing of the Civil War without being in the central current of literature will sink under the burden. We do not want him to tell us what really happened; historians will do that far better. The poet should lead us rapidly hither and thither; he should not hesitate to use his invention or to have recourse to the intervention of the gods, so that we may rather gain the impression of a soul not mistress of herself but inspired by a divine frenzy than of a witness giving his careful evidence in a court of justice.[1]

Eumolpus proceeds to illustrate his meaning by reciting 295 verses of his own composition, in which he had rewritten the opening section of the 'Pharsalia' according to the traditional method. The gods of Olympus are introduced; and more or less direct events. Venus, Mercury, and Mars are on the side of Caesar; Apollo, Diana, Hercules, and Mercury are Pompeians. But the only result of the experiment is to convince the reader how right Lucan was to dispense with this antiquated machinery, especially in a subject so modern; how superfluous in accounting for the motives of the various actors in the drama is the hypothesis of divine suggestion; and how by that hypothesis the human interest of the story is diminished.

The attack on the schools of rhetoric in the first chapter of what is left to us of the book is more effective. A sensible protest is there made

---

[1] *Sat.* 118.

against the emptiness of the teaching in such
places. The themes of declamation, the writer
declares, are ridiculous and impossible ; the good
literature of the past is entirely neglected ; the
great object is to achieve smartness of phrase and
an appearance of brilliancy however unrelated these
may be to the realities of life ; the whole is neglected
for the parts : in fact, he concludes, so soon as
eloquence began to be studied as an art and taught
by rule of thumb, men ceased to be eloquent—
just as a man who spends much time in the kitchen
will not be savoury. Whatever takes the fancy
of boys is unlikely to be really fine, yet it is
exactly that which is most admired and studied
in the schools. Quintilian said the same thing
of Seneca when he expressed his regret that one
who could do all that he pleased should so often
through lack of judgment be pleased to do what
was not worth doing, for that if judgment had
been added to his other gifts, instead of being the
delight of boys he might have won the approval
of men of taste.[1]

The year 58 was illustrated by the victories
of Corbulo over the Parthians in Armenia. The
successes of this able commander, who had restored
the almost ruined discipline of the forces under
his command, were recognised by the Senate after
their usual manner in decrees for statues and
triumphal arches to the emperor under whose
auspices they were achieved. In the same year
Seneca incurred a certain degree of unpopularity
in connection with the trial and condemnation
of Publius Suilius. This man had been a notable

[1] Quintilian, x. 1.

informer under Claudius, and the chief instrument of Messalina's cruelty. He it was who, at the instance of the Court, brought the charges which proved fatal to Julia, daughter of Drusus, Valerius Asiaticus, Lupus, and many others. He had, in fact, been the Fouquier Tinville of the worst years of Claudius ; and as such was particularly odious to the humane Seneca to whom the death of no Roman citizen during his term of power has been imputed by any historian. After the death of Claudius and the change of system, Suilius showed no penitence for his misdeeds—preferring, says Tacitus, the reputation of a criminal to the attitude of a suppliant. In the year 58 he was prosecuted under the *lex Cincia* for having accepted fees as an advocate beyond the legal limit. The charge itself was unfair, for the law was obsolete and had been habitually disregarded ; but his adversaries were resolved that Suilius should not altogether escape the penalty of his misdeeds, and their impatience would not suffer them to await the issue of the indictment for peculation and oppression in his government of Asia which, also brought against him, could not, owing to difficulties in collecting evidence, be proceeded with for a year. Suilius, in no wise abashed, retorted by accusations against Seneca which, reported by Tacitus, and repeated with amplifications by Dion or his abbreviator, Xiphilinus, have been accepted with too ready a credence by later historians.

Seneca [he said], who had been most justly exiled by Claudius, could never forgive that prince's friends. He had passed his life in futile controversies that amused the inexperience of youth ; and was envious of those who had kept burning the torch of living and uncorrupted eloquence in the defence of their fellow-citizens. He (Suilius) had been quaestor to Germanicus ; but Seneca had stained the honour of that prince's house. Was it worse to accept a fee for honourable work from a client who was ready to give it, or to corrupt the virtue of royal women ? Was it virtue and the maxims of philosophy that taught him to accumulate so vast a fortune in four years of Court favour ? At Rome he had drawn in legacies as with a net ; the provinces were exhausted by his usuries.

The language of the old accuser was reported to Seneca with exaggerations, and did not incline him to indulgence. The trial was pressed on, and conducted before the emperor himself. Suilius pleaded that all he did was by order of Claudius, but Nero interrupted him to say that he had ascertained from his father's notes that no accusation had been commanded by him. Then Suilius alleged the commands of Messalina, but was asked why he alone was chosen to give his voice and services to the tyrant ? In the end a part of his goods was confiscated, and he himself banished to the Balearic islands, where he is said to have passed the remainder of his life in great comfort. His son Nerulinus, who was shortly afterwards prosecuted, was acquitted at the instance of the emperor. Seneca has been charged with vindictiveness on this occasion, yet if times and circumstances are taken into account, we may rather wonder at the mildness of the vengeance which a powerful minister thought it sufficient to exact from such an adversary.

CHAPTER VIII

THE power of Seneca, whose position had been
in some degree shaken by the attacks of Suilius,
was threatened at about the same time by a
more formidable antagonist. Poppaea Sabina,
beautiful, charming, nobly born, rich, and intelli-
gent, concealed beneath a modest exterior a cold
heart, a calculating disposition, and a total lack
of scruple. She was married to the brilliant and
dissipated Otho, one of the chief friends of Nero
and ornaments of his Court, after having been
divorced from a former husband, Crispinus. Otho,
whether from imprudence or ambition, vaunted
the charms of his wife to the emperor, and would
often, when about to rejoin her after dining at the
palace, describe in glowing terms the happiness
to which he was returning. The natural result
followed. Poppaea was presented to Nero, and at
first affected to be deeply smitten by his beauty
while awed by his greatness. But when the
emperor proceeded to make her his addresses
she changed her tone, spoke of her duty to Otho,
and contrasted that courtier's liberality and

magnifice: :e with the poorness of spirit shown
in Nero's devotion to Acte the freedwoman, with
whom she scorned to enter into competition.
Otho was banished from the Court and in some
danger of his life, but finally Nero, through the
interposition of Seneca, sent him out as governor
to Lusitania, where, like Petronius in Bithynia, he
proved by the excellence of his administration
that his extravagance and debauchery in Rome
had been due rather to the lack of any more
rational outlet for his activity than to a vicious
disposition. That he was capable of magnanimity
he showed in the last scene of his life ; and his
friendship for Seneca, of which Plutarch speaks,
stands to his credit.[1]

There were many complaints in this year of
the rapacity and injustice of the farmers of the
taxes ; and in consequence the total abolition
of customs duties was seriously debated in Nero's
Council. This drastic proposal having been
abandoned other measures were taken. In order
to secure that no more money should be raised
than was needed for public purposes, an edict was
issued that the nature of each tax and the principles
on which it was collected, which had hitherto
been kept secret, should be published by the
tax-gatherers, and that no demand should be
made later than a year after a tax had become
due. In the assessment of a merchant's possessions for purposes of taxation, his ships were not

---

[1] He remained for ten years governor of Lusitania, returning
in 68 for the stormy three months' reign which was ended by his
defeat and death. Tac. *Ann*. xiii. 45 ; Suet. *Otho*, 3.

to be taken into account. Observance of these excellent proviṣions did not long outlast the power of Seneca and Burrhus.

The following year (59) brought with it the definite emancipation of Nero, and the consequent decline of good government. Although the emperor hated his mother, although he exercised his ingenuity to contrive mortifications for her to the point of hiring bravoes to shout insults from their boats as they sailed past her villa on the Campanian coast, he could never overcome the awe with which she inspired him, and when she met him face to face she could always bend him to submission. Agrippina was therefore an obstacle to the ambitious designs of Poppaea, who knew that while she lived Nero would never dare to discard Octavia and marry herself. Scandalous rumours were abroad and widely credited, that Agrippina was endeavouring to preserve her power by inviting her son to incest ; while a minority declared that the horrible suggestion proceeded from Nero himself. In any case Acte, prompted by Seneca, brought these rumours to the notice of the emperor, with the intimation that if they gained credit among the soldiers there would be a mutiny. Nero, greatly alarmed and already moved by the persistent taunts of Poppaea, resolved to rid himself of his mother ; and, his first attempts to poison her having been foiled by the precautionary measures of the experienced empress, cast about for other means.

Anicetus, a freedman in command of the fleet at Misenum and an enemy of Agrippina, suggested the expedient that was adopted. He offered to supply a vessel so constructed that at a given signal the roof of the principal cabin might be made to fall in, and the ship itself to sink through the opening of a hole in the bottom. The contrivance being approved, Nero wrote a letter to his mother couched in terms of humility and submission, in which he prayed for a reconciliation, and invited her to meet him at Baiae. Agrippina went rejoicing, was received with loving effusion, nobly entertained, placed above her son at table, treated at first with the affectionate lightness, ease, and familiarity natural to a young man in conversation with his mother, and afterwards to her yet greater satisfaction gravely consulted on matters of State, until the hour came at last for her departure.   Then Nero embraced her with extraordinary warmth, and seemed unable to detach his gaze from her countenance.

It was a fine starlight night, and the sea was calm when Agrippina went on board the gaily decorated ship that had been prepared for her. She was sitting in her cabin with a maid and Gallus, one of her suite, when, soon after the ship had left the harbour, part of the ceiling fell in and crushed Gallus to death.   The empress and her attendant, Acerronia, however escaped all hurt ; and, the mechanism through which a leak was to have been simultaneously sprung having failed to act, those of the sailors who were in the secret endeavoured to capsize the boat by bringing all weight to bear on one side. Agrippina and Acerronia were thrown into the sea, where Acerronia either attempted to save herself at her mistress's expense, or else her mistress at her own—it must ever be doubtful which—by crying out that she was the empress, and calling for help for the emperor's mother. Thereupon she was beaten to death by the oars of the sailors. Agrippina swam for her life, and was rescued by a boat from the shore. Returned to her villa, reflection on the circumstances convinced her both that a crime had been attempted and that she must conceal her suspicions. She therefore sent a messenger to Nero to inform him of the grave danger she had been in, and to relieve his anxiety on her account by the assurance that, except for a slight blow on the shoulder, she had sustained no injury. She begged him not to come to her for the present, though she knew his impulse would be to come, for what she needed most of all for her recovery was complete rest and quiet.

Nero was terrified by the news that his attempt had failed. His guilty imagination pictured the daughter of Germanicus full of rage, rousing the soldiers, arming slaves, and proclaiming her wrongs to Senate and people. He sent for Seneca and Burrhus, told them all that had happened, and asked their advice. They had none to give. But Anicetus was not at the end of his resources. He had already contrived to slip a dagger between the feet of Agrippina's messenger while he was performing his commission. The man was seized, accused of having been sent by Agrippina to assassinate the emperor, and promptly executed. Anicetus now proposed to slay the empress in her villa, and to give out that she had destroyed herself on hearing that her plot to take her son's life had failed. Nero eagerly agreed to this proposal, and the deed was done.

Matricide, even in the Rome of the first century, was thought an enormous crime ; and Nero dreaded the effect of the news on public opinion. Had his first contrivance proved successful and the death of Agrippina seemed the result of an accident at sea, it had been his intention to express sorrow for her loss and to honour her memory in the customary manner with altars and temples. As it was he knew not what to expect, and was appalled by a sense of the magnitude of a crime which, had it passed unsuspected by others, would have probably given his seared conscience no uneasiness. But the next morning he was encouraged by the flattery of the military officers, who came at the suggestion of Burrhus, to congratulate him on his escape from the dagger of Agrippina's emissary. The neighbouring towns of Campania followed suit by sending delegates to felicitate the emperor and by offering sacrifices of thanksgiving in their temples. Nero himself affected, out of grief for his mother's loss, almost to regret his own escape ; but he could no longer endure the sight of Baiae and came to Naples, from which place he sent a letter to the Senate composed for him by Seneca. In this letter, after relating how one of Agrippina's confidential freedmen had been surprised in his presence armed with a dagger, and how the empress on the miscarriage of her attempt against his life had taken her own, he proceeded to an indictment of the whole of his mother's career. He dwelt on the atrocities of the reign of Claudius, and insinuated her responsibility for them ; he recalled her ambition to be his colleague in the Empire and to receive in his company the oath of allegiance ; and asserted that on her failure to achieve this object she had opposed all donatives to soldiers or people. He was obliged, he added, to recognise, however great his natural grief for her loss might be, that her death was a public benefit.[1] The letter deceived nobody. No one could believe that the wreck was an accident or that Agrippina would have been mad enough to send a single individual to attack the emperor in the midst of his guards. The character of Nero was already so well known that no fresh infamy on his part could any longer cause surprise; but the composition of the letter by Seneca was the subject of hostile criticism, and was not only regarded at the time by his enemies as an avowal of complicity in the murder, but has weighed more heavily on his memory ever since than any other incident in his career. Yet that Seneca and Burrhus were the accomplices or advisers of Nero's plot to murder his mother is in a high degree improbable; it is unlike all we know of their characters ; and, as the event proved, such advice would have

---

[1] In this letter occurred the ingenious phrase afterwards quoted by Quintilian as an example of a form of the *sententia* : ' Facit quasdam sententias sola geminatio : qualis est Senecae in eo scripto quod Nero ad Senatum misit occisa matre, cum se periclitatum videri vellet : " Salvum me esse adhuc nec credo nec gaudeo " ' (Quint. viii. 5).

been as unwise from the standpoint of their own interests as wicked from every other. After the deed had been done, Seneca probably convinced himself that there was nothing better to do than to make the best of a bad situatioh, and that if to desert his post, to abandon Burrhus, and to leave the Empire to the mercies of Nero would be an unpatriotic course, the only alternative was, not to condone the crime, but to deny that a crime had been committed. ' What better proof can a man give of devotion to virtue,' he wrote in one of his letters, ' than a readiness to sacrifice reputation itself for conscience' sake ? '[1] Yet when all is said, the letter to the Senate remains of all the recorded actions of Seneca the least defensible.

Nero might have spared himself anxiety with regard to the Senate. The chief preoccupation of that assembly at this crisis was to show the unqualified nature of their submission to the autocrat. Decrees were passed for thanksgivings to the gods at every shrine ; for the annual cele-bration of the day on which the supposed plot had been frustrated ; and for the erection of a golden statue to Minerva to be placed next to that of the prince in the senate-house. Thrasea Paetus, who up to that time had acquiesced in silence or in a few formal words to decrees passed in honour of Nero, refused further compliance and, declining to assent to these new compliments on such an occasion, withdrew from the senate-house, to which he but seldom returned. ' His action,' observes Tacitus drily, ' though full of danger to

[1] *Ep.* 81.

himself was of no service to the cause of liberty.'[1]
Nor were the people to be outdone in their
manifestations of loyalty to the prince—a loyalty
which with them was not wholly feigned, for
Nero's lavish bounties, his shows, and popular
manners had made him a favourite with the mob,
while Agrippina, on the other hand, had been very
unpopular. When, therefore, after an unusually
long stay in Campania, he nerved himself to
return to Rome, he was received with an enthusiasm which far surpassed his most sanguine
hopes, and made a triumphant entry into the city.
This experience convinced him that he might do
what he would with impunity ; and from this
time forward he gave free play to the boundless
intemperance of his vicious will.

Nero was inordinately vain of his voice and of
his performances on the lute. That his musical
genius should be universally recognised was his
chief ambition, and he longed to appear on the
public stage there to win applause such as had
been given to no other performer. He was wont
to justify his passion for song and music by the
example of a god honoured not only in Greece
but in Rome, with whom the poets of his time
never wearied of comparing him.[2] And song, he

---

[1] In making this remark the historian may have had in mind
his own contrasted conduct under the tyranny of Domitian,
during which he continued to attend the Senate and with bitterness in his heart shared in all its degradation.

[2] Senec. *Apoc.* : ' Ille mihi similis vultu similisque decore,
Nec cantu nec voce minor.' Lucan, *Phars.* i. 48–50 : ' Seu te flam-
miferos Phoebi transcendere currus, Telluremque, nihil mutato
sole timentem, Igne vago lustrare juvat.' Cf. also eclogues in
Anthologia Latina of Riese, 725 and 726.

would argue with some justice, is nothing without an audience.[1] But Phoebus was not only the god of music, he was the charioteer of the sun ; and here also he was followed by the emperor. For Nero's second passion was the management of horses in chariots; his skill in which he was almost as anxious to exhibit to the public as the beauty of his voice. While, however, his mother lived he shrank from degrading the majesty of the Caesars by the self-exposure involved in public exhibitions. He hated Agrippina, but he dreaded her contempt.[2]

After the death of Agrippina, Seneca and Burrhus found it impossible longer to resist the prince's inclinations. In the hope, therefore, that by a compromise they might satisfy his vanity while averting a public scandal, they caused a space of level ground at the foot of the Palatine hill to be enclosed on which Nero might exhibit his skill as a charioteer to a selected audience. But vanity, like jealousy, is a passion that makes the meat it feeds on ; and the only effect on Nero of the applause of his friends was to make him hunger for a larger circle of spectators. Barriers were cast aside and the Roman people invited to the spectacle. The populace, delighted to see

[1] Suet. *Nero*, 20 : ' Jactans occultae musicae nullum esse respectum.'

[2] It has been thought remarkable, and a proof of their hardness of heart, that the Romans were more shocked by Nero's stage performances than by his cruelties or debaucheries. But if we consider what would have been the effect in modern times on the minds of their subjects of the appearance of a German or a Russian emperor on the public stage of the opera in female costume we shall feel less surprise.

their emperor personally contributing to their favourite amusement, were loud in their plaudits ; while the ministers found to their distress that in endeavouring to direct and control they had only fanned the flame of Nero's folly. To cover his shame he persuaded the noblest youth of Rome to follow his example, and rewarded with large sums of money those of them whose poverty if not their will consented.

But though Nero had performed before the public as a charioteer, he did not as yet venture to appear in the theatre as a singer or actor. For *mimes*, for all exhibitions of a man's person or physical accomplishments with a view to the public entertainment, the Romans had a contempt unparalleled in any nation ancient or modern. Self-exposure of any kind they condemned as a violation of that *pudor* which they ranked so high among the virtues. Nero was a poet and musician as well as a singer. He could sing his own poems to the accompaniment of his own lyre and music of his own composition, and he was resolved not to hide his talents. With this end in view he instituted the *juvenalia*, or festivals of the youth, to consist of musical and dramatic performances. These were privately celebrated from time to time in the emperor's palace gardens, and were accompanied by much profligacy and debauchery. They were attended by the Court, together with men and women of noble birth and of all ages, many of whom shared in the performances. Here, for the first time, Nero appeared on the boards in costume, lyre in hand, to sing songs which were greeted with rapturous applause. A group of Roman knights, taking the name of *Augustani*, formed themselves into a society, the sole object of which was to applaud the emperor and to proclaim the glory of the ' divine voice.' Burrhus himself, with the officers of the guard, was reluctantly obliged to be present and to join in the applause.[1] As Tacitus makes no mention of Seneca in this connection, we may perhaps infer that the philosopher excused himself from attendance.

[1] *Ann.* xiv. 15 : ' Centuriones tribunique et maerens Burrhus et laudans.'

H

CHAPTER IX

DECLINE OF SENECA'S INFLUENCE—DEATH
OF BURRHUS AND OF OCTAVIA, A.D. 60-62

IN spite of Nero's growing self-confidence and
impatience of control, his aversion from business
secured two more years of relatively wise and
humane administration to Rome after the death
of Agrippina. Until his vanity, that 'insatiate
cormorant,' had consumed the vast resources
left for its satisfaction by the economies of his
predecessor, he was under no temptation to
resort to oppression for its further supply. The
law of *majestas* had been suffered to become
obsolete ; informers had been discouraged ;
governors of provinces had been made to give a
strict account of their stewardship, and punished
when they deserved it ; and the popularity which
these wise measures of his ministers brought
to the prince was more than doubled by the
extravagance of his shows and his lavish dis-
tributions of presents to the people.

The chief event at Rome of the year 60 was
the solemn institution by Nero of quinquennial
games, consisting of gymnastic and musical contests, and also of chariot racing—destined to be

continued at intervals of five years for centuries. A festival of this kind, copied from a Greek model, was a novelty to the Romans, who had been accustomed to profess a singular contempt for the athletic and artistic achievements held in such honour by the Greeks.[1] There were mutterings from conservatives, who deplored the State encouragement of Greek accomplishments unworthy of Romans; but these were answered by the upholders of modern ideas, who dwelt on the relief to the magistrates, ruined by the expense of the shows they were obliged to provide for the people out of their private means, when a part of this expense should be defrayed from the public purse; and also on the stimulus to intellectual activity which the prizes at these contests for poetry and eloquence would supply. The first celebration of the *Neronia*, as the games were called, was decently conducted. The prize for eloquence was not competed for but formally allotted to Nero.

The following year (61) was rendered memorable by the disaster in Britain, where 70,000 Romans are said to have been massacred in a sudden rising of the inhabitants under their warrior queen, Boadicea. The rising was suppressed by the energy and ability of the governor, Suetonius Paullinus. Nero had no liking for successful commanders, and Suetonius was rewarded for his victory by his recall.

[1] Lucan, vii. 270: ' Graiis delecta juventus Gymnasiis aderit, studioque ignava palaestrae.' Tac., *Ann.* xiv. 20: 'Degeneretque studiis externis juventus, gymnasia et otia et turpes amores exercendo, Principe et Senatu auctoribus.'

In Rome the event of the year which excited the greatest interest was the murder of Pedanius Secundus, prefect of the city, by one of his own slaves, because of the demand which followed it for the enforcement of the old law under which when a master was killed by a slave all the other slaves of the household as well as himself were put to death. The people had grown accustomed to a milder régime, and the proposed punishment of so large a number of their fellow-men of both sexes and of every age nearly caused a revolt. Even in the Senate a minority protested against the application of so severe a law. The writings of Seneca, the most widely read author of the day, in which he pleaded the cause of slaves, insisted on their common humanity, called them ' humble friends ' and fellow-servants of fortune, and laughed at those who held it degrading to sit at table in their company, may have had some effect on public opinion.[1] Tacitus has preserved for us a speech made in the Senate by one Caius Cassius, in which we have the judgment of a Roman senator of the old school on the new ideas, full of false sentiment and degenerate softness as he would think them, which found their leading exponent in the treatises of Seneca :—

I have very often been present, Patres Conscripti, in this assembly when proposals have been made

---

[1] *Ep.* 47 : ' Servi sunt ? imo homines. Servi sunt ? imo contubernales. Servi sunt ? imo humiles amici. Servi sunt ? imo conservi, si cogitaveris tantundem in utrosque licere fortunae. Itaque rideo istos qui turpe existimant cum servo suo coenare : quare ? nisi quia superbissima consuetudo coenanti domino stantium servorum turbam circumdedit.'

contrary to the laws and institutions of our ancestors, and I have raised no opposition. This was not because I doubted at any time the wisdom and right policy of our ancient institutions, or supposed they could be altered except for the worse ; but, in the first place, because I would not in my zeal for the old order appear to attach too much importance to my own opinion ; and, in the second place, because a continual course of opposition in matters of lesser moment is apt to weaken the force of our resistance at times when the highest interests of the commonwealth are threatened. Consider what has just happened. A man of consular rank has been killed in his own house by a treacherous slave. No one interfered to save him or revealed the plot, and that although the law under which the whole family became responsible for his safety had not yet been called into question. Pass then, in the name of heaven, your act of indemnity. Whose rank will protect him when the prefecture of the city is of no avail ? How many slaves shall we need for our defence when four hundred could not secure the safety of Pedanius ? : . . Some there are who are not ashamed to pretend that the assassin was avenging the wrongs he had suffered because he was himself being robbed. Let us say at once, then, that Pedanius was justly slain ! Would you have me find arguments for enforcing a law established long ago by wiser men than we ? Well, then, I will suppose that it is a question of passing it for the first time, and I ask you whether it is credible that a slave should have formed the intention of killing his master and given no hint to any of his design by a single rash or threatening word ? He concealed his plot very successfully forsooth ; no one saw his weapon ; he passed the guard ; he opened the doors of the bed-chamber ; he passed in bearing a torch ; he committed the murder ; and no one was aware of what he was doing ! It is impossible. . . . Our ancestors mistrusted the disposition of slaves, even when born in their own houses or on their estates and therefore bound to them by lifelong ties of affection and gratitude. But now when households are made up from distant nations, when we have slaves whose manners and religion differ so widely from our own, we can certainly never keep this vile multitude in order except by working on their fears. The innocent, it is said, will perish with the guilty. Why, so they do in a defeated army, when every tenth man is beaten to death; the lot may fall on the brave. Something of injustice you will find in every great example; but the interests of individuals must be sacrificed to the general good.

No senator was bold enough openly to oppose the views of Cassius, and, though dissentient murmurs were heard condemning the mockery of justice that took neither sex nor age nor patent innocence into account, it was resolved that the law should be enforced. Riots ensued among the populace, and a threat of resistance was uttered. Thereupon the imperial displeasure was proclaimed by edict, the road from the prison to the place of execution was lined with soldiers, and the four hundred slaves, men, women, and children, were put to death.

The year 62 opened ominously with the revival of the law of *majestas*, or treason, which had lain dormant since the death of Claudius. At a banquet given at the house of Ostorius Scapula the praetor Antistius, one of the guests, recited some scurrilous verses of his own composition against the emperor. Cossutius Capito, who had been raised to senatorial rank by the influence of his father-in-law, Tigellinus, accused Antistius of treason before the Senate. Ostorius declared that he had heard no verses recited, but credit

was given to the evidence of other witnesses, and
Junius Marullus, consul designate, moved that
Antistius should be deprived of his praetorship
and put to death in the ancient fashion. But
Thrasea Paetus rose to oppose this motion, and,
after much praise of Caesar and reproaches
addressed to Antistius, declared that savage
punishments such as that demanded belonged
to another age, and that the laws allowed the
adoption of milder alternatives. He therefore
moved that Antistius should be punished by the
confiscation of his property and banishment to
an island. This motion was carried on a division ;
but, before venturing to give effect to it, the consuls
thought it prudent to ask counsel of the emperor.
Nero, offended and embarrassed, replied that he
had been attacked without a cause by Antistius,
who certainly deserved to be punished. For
the rest, had the Senate decided on the severer
penalty, he should have interfered to prevent its
infliction, but he could make no objection to their
moderation. Indeed, they might acquit the
prisoner altogether if they so pleased. In spite
of the manifest annoyance of the emperor, the
Senate did not recede from their vote ; some of
them, says Tacitus, in order not to expose the
prince to unpopularity, others perceiving safety
in numbers, and Thrasea out of his natural greatness of soul. This was perhaps the last occasion
during Nero's reign on which the Senate showed
independence.

The death of Burrhus, which soon followed,
dealt a shattering blow to Seneca's power and

influence for good. It is to the credit of both men that the friendship and union between them had remained throughout unbroken by any sentiment of rivalry or jealousy ; and, while the military force was under the command of Burrhus, Nero did not venture to rid himself of Seneca. Burrhus was succeeded in the command of the Praetorians by Tigellinus, the most profligate and corrupt of Nero's associates, with whom as a concession to public opinion was joined as a colleague Fenius Rufus—an honest man, liked by the soldiers and respected by the people on account of the integrity with which he had administered the distribution of corn. But Rufus was given no real power, while Tigellinus, on the other hand, who had cultivated a good understanding with Poppaea, acquired a predominant influence over the emperor, whose worst impulses he encouraged.

After the death of Burrhus the enemies of Seneca redoubled their attacks, to which they perceived that the emperor was beginning to listen with scarcely veiled satisfaction. With the exaggeration customary in all ages when the fortunes of public men are in question, they dwelt on the extent of his revenues too vast for a subject, the number of his villas, and the beauty of his gardens, almost surpassing in magnificence, so they said, those of the emperor himself. They accused him, probably with more justice, of depreciating Nero's skill as a charioteer, and of openly deriding the celestial voice. They insinuated that he claimed a monopoly of eloquence, that so soon as Nero had begun to write poetry his own poetical activity had been found to increase, and that, in fact, he would allow nothing of eloquence to appear in the republic that did not proceed from himself. Nero, they said, had passed his childhood; let him shake off his yoke, and show that he needed no other guidance than that supplied him by the example of his ancestors.

The appointment of Tigellinus to the post of Burrhus convinced Seneca that he could be of no further service to the State, and he became anxious to retire from public life. But it was no easy matter to withdraw from the service of the suspicious Nero. Seneca himself in one of his letters, with the worldly wisdom which he commonly blends with his philosophy, observed that it is dangerous to seem to seek a safe retreat, since a man implicitly condemns that which he shuns.[1] However, he obtained an audience, and on the plea of age and growing infirmities begged to be allowed to retire from the Court and devote the short remainder of his life to his studies. At the same time he entreated the prince to come to his assistance by allowing him to restore to his imperial benefactor the great possessions which he owed to his munificence. But Nero would not accept his resignation or the proffered sacrifice of his gardens and villas. He professed the highest value for the services of his minister, loaded him with caresses, and dismissed him with tender reproaches that he

---

[1] *Ep.* xiv. : 'Sapiens nocituram potentiam vitat, hoc primum cavens, ne vitare videatur. Pars enim securitatis et in hoc est, non ex professo eam petere ; quia quae quis fugit damnat.'

should be content to gain credit for disinterestedness at the risk of exposing his friend to the suspicion of avarice, and that he should desire a retirement which would be interpreted as fear of Nero's cruelty. Seneca thanked the prince and withdrew ; but from that time forth changed his whole manner of life ; discontinued his receptions of clients, spent little time abroad and avoided all society, devoting himself in seclusion to his studies, and writing his immortal letters to Lucilius. The change in the direction of affairs soon made itself felt. Burrhus, Tigellinus told Nero, had other interests ; but for himself, the emperor's safety was the one object. He endeavoured to alarm Nero with reports of conspiracies, and to plunge him into crime in order to secure his own position as an indispensable guardian and accomplice. Rubellius Plautus and Cornelius Sulla were the first victims of this system. Plautus was a descendant through his mother of Augustus. He had adopted Stoic principles and, though a man of vast possessions, the simplicity and dignity of his domestic life had won him universal respect. Two years previously, in the year 61, when the appearance of a comet, a slight illness of the emperor, and other signs had made many people believe that a change was imminent, he had been spoken of as a candidate for the Empire· Thereupon Nero had sent him a letter in which he suggested that, in order to silence these invidious reports for which he did not hold him responsible, it might be well that he should retire for a time to his ancestral estates in the province of Asia, and there live out his youth free from danger or intrigue. Plautus complied, and was still living in the province when the death of Burrhus and the partial retirement of Seneca brought Tigellinus into power. Cornelius Sulla, a dull man, whose only importance was derived from his descent from the dictator, had been living in exile at Marseilles since the year 58, whither he had been sent on a trumped-up accusation of a plot against the emperor, of which no one who knew his indolent disposition believed him to be capable.

Tigellinus, closely studying the humours of his master, discovered that these two men were the living fears in Nero's heart, and thereupon urged, as from himself, their destruction. Nero at once agreed, and on the sixth day after emissaries sent for the purpose had left Rome, Sulla was assassinated while dining at Marseilles and his head brought back to the emperor, who laughed at the premature whiteness of the hair on it. The execution of Plautus was a more dangerous business. Unlike Sulla, he had many friends and great possessions. He was warned of his danger by a despatch from his father-in-law, Antistius, who urged him to resistance. But Plautus was a Stoic philosopher and a fatalist, and he thought the doubtful chance of a longer life not worth the struggle, while he hoped that his submission might incline the emperor to a better treatment of his wife and children. Nero's assassin found him at noon stripped for the exercises of his gymnasium. Here he was slain, and his head, like that of Sulla, brought back to

the exulting tyrant.   An imperial message to the
Senate made no direct mention of the deaths of
Plautus and Sulla, but spoke vaguely of their
factious disposition and the emperor's constant
watchfulness over the public safety.   They were
thereupon expelled from the Senate and the usual
supplications decreed.

These crimes were followed by the murder
of the innocent and unhappy Octavia.   This
princess, whose brief life had been but one series
of calamities unredeemed by a single gleam of
happiness, was adored by the people, who com-
miserated her misfortunes and detested her rival
Poppaea.   Nero began by divorcing her on the
ground of sterility, and removed her first to
a house once inhabited by Burrhus and afterwards into Campania, where she was placed under
a military guard.   She was next charged with
adultery with an Egyptian slave; but the heroic
constancy of her waiting-maids, who continued
under torture to declare her innocence, made it
necessary to abandon this charge, and the emperor,
intimidated by popular clamour, decided to recall her.   Great rejoicings followed ; the statues
of Poppaea were thrown down, and those of
Octavia adorned with flowers.   The multitude
advanced towards the palace to express their
gratitude to the emperor, but they were met by
a charge from the soldiers and dispersed with
bloodshed.   Poppaea, assisted by Tigellinus, used
all her wiles to restore Nero's resolution and to
compass the ruin of Octavia.   The services of
Anicetus, the murderer of Agrippina, were again

called into requisition. This man had become odious to Nero, on the principle that ' they love not poison that do poison need,' and was ready for any new crime to recover his favour. He agreed to accuse himself of being the lover of Octavia, and exceeded his instructions in the shamelessness of his pretended disclosures. After his statement made to Nero's council he was removed to Sardinia, and there enabled to spend the remaining years of his miserable life in physical comfort. Octavia, still but in her twentieth year, having witnessed the murders of her father and brother by a husband who had hated and cruelly treated her from the first day of their pretended union, was now confined in fetters in the island of Pandataria, and after a few days put to death. Her head was brought to her cruel rival, Poppaea, whose marriage to Nero had immediately followed the divorce.

In the following year (63) Poppaea gave birth to a daughter, and Nero was beside himself with joy. The Senate fell in with his mood and voted temples, thanksgivings to the gods, and honours to the child and mother, with their customary subservience. The child was born at Antium—Nero's own birthplace—and thither the senators went to offer their congratulations — all except Thrasea, whose absence drew a bitter comment from the emperor. Afterwards Nero boasted to Seneca that he had reconciled himself to Thrasea. A flatterer would have replied with the anticipated protest against such an excess of magnanimity, but Seneca merely expressed himself

delighted at the news and offered his congratulations—a reply, comments Tacitus, much to his
honour and to that of Thrasea, but fraught with
peril to both these excellent men. The child
itself died in four months' time and Nero, excessive
in all things, abandoned himself to the wildest
manifestations of grief, which the divine honours
voted to his lost treasure by a sympathetic Senate
were powerless to assuage.

CHAPTER X

SENECA IN RETIREMENT—HIS FRIENDS AND OCCUPATIONS

DURING the last three years of his life Seneca occupied himself as little as he could with public affairs. The emperor would not consent to his formal retreat, and still occasionally consulted him, but he lived at Rome as little as possible, making his health an excuse for spending most of his time in one or other of his villas. In his retirement, which he shared with his young wife Paullina, to whom he was tenderly attached, Seneca occupied himself with reading, writing, self-examination, meditation on the nature of things, and researches into natural history. His book of *Naturales Quaestiones*, written in the last year of his life, was the result of these researches in which, says Quintilian, he was sometimes misled by those whom he employed to make investigations. This book, though without scientific value, assumes the existence of natural causes for all phenomena however unusual, and rejects the notion that they were special indications of the divine purpose, or bore any but accidental relation to human destiny.[1]

Seneca was also an expert vine-grower, and his vineyard at Nomentum was the admiration of Italian agriculturists.[2] The territory of Nomentum, a small and ancient town in the neighbourhood of Rome, was celebrated for its vineyards. A new system of cultivation had been introduced there with very successful results by a freedman named Acilius Sthenelus. The methods of Sthenelus were imitated by the well-known grammarian Palaemon, a man of infamous morals and inordinate vanity, but whose energy and ability had raised him from the condition of a slave to wealth and high distinction in his profession.[3] Palaemon bought at a low price some neglected land at Nomentum, and set to work to grow vines on it according to the system of Sthenelus. He succeeded so well that within eight years his vineyards had become an object of interest to all men engaged in vine-growing, and the proximity of Nomentum to Rome brought him a stream of visitors by which his vanity—

---

[1] *Nat. Quaest.* vi. 3 : 'Illud quoque proderit praesumere animo, nihil horum deos facere ; nec ira numinum, aut caelum concuti, aut terram. Suas ista causas habent : nec ex imperio saeviunt, sed ex quibusdam vitiis, ut corpora nostra, turbantur : et tunc, cum facere videntur, injuriam accipiunt.'

[2] *Nat. Quaest.* iii. 7 : 'Ego tibi vinearum diligens fossor affirmo.' Pliny, xiv. 4 : 'Annaeo Seneca . . . tanto praedii ejus amore capto, ut non puderet inviso alias et ostentaturo tradere palmam eam, emptis quadruplicato vineis illis intra decennium fere curae annum.' Columella, iii. 3.

[3] Nevertheless, in the expressed opinion of both the emperors Tiberius and Claudius his moral character unfitted him to be placed in charge of youth.

the leading motive, according to Pliny, of all his activities—must have been abundantly gratified. Among the rest came Seneca, who was so charmed with what he saw that he purchased the property at a price four times as large as that which Palaemon had paid for it less than ten years previously. The farm did not suffer from the change of ownership. Columella, a contemporary, writes that in his time the vineyards of Nomentum were celebrated for their excellence, and that the best yield of all was from that belonging to Seneca.[1]

The practical character of Seneca's philosophy, his love of tangible results, his constant desire to penetrate through appearances to realities, render comprehensible his taste for agriculture. A rival vine-grower, mentioned by Pliny, was Vetalinus Aegialus, by origin a freedman, who lived on an estate in the district of Liternum, in Campania, formerly occupied by Scipio Africanus during his exile from Rome. Seneca visited him there, and has left in one of his letters an interesting description of the house and olive plantations, with a detailed account of the various methods of planting and transplanting olive-trees and vines :

I am writing you [Lucilius] this letter from the actual house of Scipio Africanus, where I am staying, and where I have adored his ' manes ' and the coffin which I believe to contain the body of that great man . . . I find a house constructed of square stones, in a wood, surrounded

---

[1] Colum.; *De re rustica*, iii. 3 : ' Nomentana regio celeberrima fama est illustris, et praecipue quam possidet Seneca, vir excellentis ingenii atque doctrinae, cujus in praediis vinearum jugera singula culleos octonos reddidisse plerumque compertum est.'

by a wall, with towers erected at each corner for its
defence.   There is a tank to supply the buildings and the
plants which might suffice for the wants of a whole army.
The small bath is rather dark, as we generally find in
baths of that time.   It gave me great pleasure to contemplate Scipio's way of living and to contrast it with
ours.   It was in this dark corner that the terror of
Carthage, to whom Rome owes it that she was captured
only once, used to bathe his body wearied with country
work, for his exercise took the form of labour, and he
used to plough his fields himself, after the manner of
the ancients.   Under this humble roof he lived ; on
this common pavement he walked.   Who now would
endure to bathe in this manner ?   A man now thinks
himself poor and mean unless his walls glisten with
large and costly marble, with Alexandrian blocks con-
trasting with Numidian, with elaborate texture of mosaic
as from a painter's hand ;   unless his arched roof is
hidden by plate glass ;   unless marble from Thasos, once
the rare and conspicuous decoration of some temple,
cover the walls of a swimming-bath into which he plunges
a body exhausted by profuse perspiration ;   unless water
flows from silver sluices.   And I am speaking only of
common baths ;   what shall be said when we come to the
baths of freedmen, with their many statues, and columns
supporting nothing but placed there merely for show, and
by reason of their costliness ?   What of the sound of waters
rushing down the steps ?   Our luxury has reached such
a pitch that the very floor on which we tread must be
set with precious stones.   In this bath of Scipio there
are chinks, hardly to be called windows, cut in the stone
wall, so that light may be admitted without weaken-
ing the defences.   But nowadays we think baths musty
unless they are contrived so as to admit the full rays
of the sun to fall through vast windows upon the bathers
and warm them as they bathe, and to enable them to
enjoy from their seats a prospect of sea and land.   New
inventions of luxury constantly outstrip the old, and
every novelty which made baths admired and run after

at the time of their dedication soon becomes out of date and out of fashion. Of old, baths were few and their arrangements simple, for there was little need for decoration when the object of bathing was cleanliness, not pleasure, and when a bath cost less than a penny. Water was not poured over the bather, nor constantly renewed as from a hot spring to clean the grease from shining bodies. But, by Heaven, it was delightful to enter those dark bathing-places when you knew that a Cato or a Fabius Maximus or one of the Cornelii had tested the water with his own hands, for the office of inspecting the public baths, of seeing that they were clean and in good order, and that the temperature was kept at the right and most healthy level, was in old days discharged by the noblest aediles. . . . What a clown would Scipio now be thought, who had no broad window-panes through which to admit the light and was not accustomed to stew in a steaming bath under the full sunshine ! The water in which he bathed was not filtered, but often cloudy, indeed after heavy rain almost muddy. But that mattered little to him, for he came to wash away sweat, not ointment. One can imagine the contemptuous comment : ' We do not envy Scipio if that was his manner of bathing.' But there is worse to come ; he did not bathe every day, for we are told by the recorders of old customs that our ancestors washed their legs and arms every day because they were stained by their work, but their whole bodies only once a week. ' Clearly they were very dirty fellows ' someone will say. Of what do you think they smelt ? Of warfare ; of labour ; of manhood. Men became fouler after elegant baths were invented. . . . To use ointment is of no use unless it is renewed twice or thrice a day, otherwise it will evaporate. People glory in these odours, as if they were natural to their bodies. If all this seems to you too severe you must ascribe it to the spirit of the house, where I have been learning from Aegialus, the present owner of the estate and the most industrious of householders, how to transplant an old plantation. This is the sort of thing we veterans should learn, we are all of us planting olive yards for the benefit of those who come after us.[1]

In another letter he describes how, when attacked by fever, he escaped from Rome to Nomentum, disregarding the anxious remonstrances of Paullina, his second wife, who thought him too ill to move, and how quickly the sight of his vines and meadows, and the enjoyment of pure air after the fetid atmosphere of the city, restored him to health. In this letter, too, he dwells with gratitude on the devoted affection of Paullina, and says that it was this that reconciled him to life. His health had become a matter of concern to himself, because it was a matter of concern to her.

For since I know that I am to her as the breath of life, I begin to be careful of myself that I may be careful of her, and I give up that indifference to fate which is the chief boon brought by old age. This old man, I tell myself, has youth in his keeping and must therefore spare himself. . . . It is sweet, moreover, to be so dear to a wife that a man becomes dearer to himself.[2]

Another villa owned by Seneca in the neighbourhood of Rome was in the Alban district, where many rich Romans possessed houses and whither the emperors themselves used to resort to their magnificent villa first occupied by Pompey, large remains of which are still visible at Albano. Seneca gives in one of his letters a characteristic account of a surprise visit he paid to his Alban villa about this time. He relates how he arrived

[1] *Ep.* 86. [2] *Ep.* 104.

late at night after a troublesome journey and found nothing ready for his reception but the contented mind he brought with him. This he owed, so he writes, to the reflections that nothing external really matters if you take it lightly; that all that is displeasing in our indignation arises from the feeling itself, not from its subject; that evil resides not in things, but in the opinion we have of them; and that although there was no bread in the house but the coarse stuff eaten by his bailiff and labourers, he would find, if he waited long enough to be hungry, that this was better than the bread to which he was accustomed. Amusing himself with these philosophical meditations he went supperless to bed, and determined to eat no scrap till his appetite should clamour for the homely fare within his reach and he could digest it with pleasure. A stomach well-disciplined and trained to put up with indignities, he moralised the next morning to Lucilius, is of the greatest use to one who would be free. He is delighted to find with what perfect unconcern he can endure unexpected inconveniences ; for, as he remarks, a man if given time can brace himself to do without many things, the sudden loss of which he would feel.

We do not understand how many of the things we use are superfluous till we begin to dispense with them. Then we find that we made use of them merely because we possessed them. With how many things we surround ourselves only because others have done the same, because it is the fashion ! A fruitful source of our errors is that we live by imitation and are guided by custom rather than by reason. When a practice of any kind is adopted but by a few we leave it alone, when more people take to it we follow suit, just as if it were better because more common, and when some extravagance becomes general we begin to think it right. For instance, no man of fashion cares to make a journey without being preceded by an escort of Numidian outriders and runners. He would despise himself if the road were not cleared for his passage and unless a great dust heralded the approach of a person of consequence, while the accoutrements of his mules must be of precious material wrought by great artists.

He goes on to warn Lucilius to avoid the insidious society of those who declare virtue and justice and philosophy to be empty names, and that to take pleasure as it flies is the only sensible course for an ephemeral being like man. Death, these say, will take all ; why then anticipate its action by the surrender of what it will take ? What madness to act as steward for your heir and so make him long for your departure, because the more you have the better pleased will he be to see you go. Reputation is a bubble, pleasure the one reality. Such siren-songs as these, says Seneca, must be shunned like the plague. They turn us from our country, from our parents, from our friends, from virtue, and dash us to pieces on a rock of degradation. No one is good by accident ; virtue is a difficult science and must be learnt. Pleasure, which we share with the animals, which attracts the meanest of created things, must be a petty and contemptible thing. Poverty is an evil only to him who declines it. Superstition is very madness ; it fears those whom it should love ; it dishonours those whom it worships. As well deny the existence of gods as report so vilely of their character. There is no hope for the sick man whom his physician urges to intemperance.[1]

One fruit of retirement, especially to Seneca's taste, was the increased opportunities which it brought him of intercourse with his friends. Throughout his life he had cultivated friendship with chosen men of every rank, and he had a high idea of all that was implied in the term.

Consider long [he writes] before admitting a man to be your friend, but when you have done so, admit him to your heart of hearts, speak as freely to him as to yourself. Do you indeed so live as to entrust nothing to yourself which you would be ashamed to confide even to an enemy; yet since there are things which we are accustomed to keep secret, share with your friend all your cares, all your thoughts. If you think him faithful you will make him so.[2]

The wise man, even if sufficient unto himself, wishes to have a friend; if on no other account yet that he may practise friendship . . . not for the reasons Epicurus gives, that he may have someone to nurse him when ill or to succour him when in prison or in want, but that he may himself have someone to nurse, or to liberate when a prisoner. He who regards himself and for his own sake seeks for friendship is in error; as it has begun, so will it end. He has prepared a friend to bring him aid when in chains, at the first clank that friend will leave him. . . . You begin a friendship for your own advantage, if a greater advantage offers you will break it, because you have looked for a reward outside itself. Wherefore do I make myself a friend? To have one for whom I can die, whom I can follow into exile, for whose life I may risk and spend my own.[3]

[1] *Ep*. 123.   [2] *Ep*. 3.   [3] *Ep*. 9.

Friendship [he writes to Lucilius] makes all things common between us, neither prosperity nor adversity can fall to our single share. We live in common. No one can live happily who looks to himself alone, who turns everything to his own profit ; you must live for another if you would live for yourself—'*alteri vivas oportet, si vis tibi vivere.*' The binding union which mingles all with all and claims that there are rights common to the whole human race must be carefully and sacredly observed. To this end the cultivation of that tie of intimate friendship I spoke of is of the greatest service, for he who shares all things with his friend will share much with mankind.[1]

The soul knows no pleasure comparable to a sweet and faithful friendship. How good it is to have one to whom you can confide every secret, whose knowledge you fear less than your own, whose conversation soothes your cares, whose judgment solves your perplexities, whose cheerfulness drives away melancholy, whose very sight enchants you.[2]

In spite of, perhaps owing to, this lofty notion of friendship, Seneca had a goodly list of friends. Nearest of all to his heart was Annaeus Serenus, captain of Nero's bodyguard, whose name suggests that he may have been a relation. To him he addressed the treatise *De Constantia Sapientis* ; and the *De Tranquillitate Animi* is in the form of a dialogue between Serenus and himself. The younger man is made to consult Seneca with respect to certain difficulties which he has encountered in his progress in philosophy. His reason has convinced him that a simple life is the best, and his real inclinations agree with his reason. Yet he finds his eyes dazzled by the

---

[1] *Ep.* 48.　　　　[2] *De Tranquill. Anim.* i. 7.

splendour he sees around him ; and he is conscious
of an occasional conflict between his moral and
physical nature, troubling him much as sea-sickness
may trouble a man though the ship is in no danger.
These weaknesses humiliate and disturb him, and
he asks Seneca to prescribe some means by which
he may gain a constant and invulnerable tranquillity of soul. Seneca in reply treats, as he
says, the whole question in order that from the
general remedy Serenus may extract what he
needs to meet his own case. His remedy, in
brief, is self-devotion to the welfare of others,
whether by public service of the State, in which a
man must regard honours only so far as they
may help him to be useful to his friends, to his
fellow-citizens, and to the whole world ; or, if
the temptations incident to such a life may not
safely be confronted, to the equally necessary
work of teaching the world the meaning of justice,
of piety, of patience, of fortitude, of the contempt
of death, of the nature of the gods, and finally,
what all may have who will, of a good conscience.
We have no power over fortune. Life is in one
sense a perpetual servitude, whatever its out-
ward aspect ; but we have power to act rightly,
however fortune may treat us, and there are no
conceivable circumstances in which we may not
secure tranquillity by serving our fellow-creatures
in the measure of our power. A discriminating
choice of friends, moderation in all things, with a
rational end kept constantly in view in all our
actions and desires, the elimination of the superfluous, the avoidance alike of anxiety and of frivolity,

achieved by constantly keeping in mind the truth
that external things being beyond our power
and subject to fortune are unimportant, to laugh
rather than weep at the follies and vices of the
multitude, recreation, and the cultivation of
cheerfulness—these are the more worldly-wise
counsels addressed to Serenus personally with
which Seneca closes his treatise.   It was written
during the *Quinquennium*, at the height of his
prosperity, and is free from the gloom, the sense
of impending tragedy, the passionate exhortations
to constancy, the tremendous seriousness which
mark his later writings when the reign of terror
had begun.

Serenus died while still young of a dish of
poisonous fungi.[1]   Of his grief at this event Seneca
afterwards wrote to Lucilius, whom he was consoling for the loss of a friend :

> Though I write thus to you, yet I myself mourned
> for my dearest friend Annaeus Serenus with such ex-
> travagance of lamentation that I am become a name
> among those who have been vanquished by sorrow—the
> last thing I desired.   Now, however, I blame myself, and
> perceive that the chief reason of my excess of grief was
> that I had never thought that he could have died before
> me.   I only reflected that he was younger, and much
> younger—as if the Fates preserved the order of age.[2]

Another of Seneca's friends of a very different
sort was Demetrius, the cynic philosopher.   Demetrius was a native of Sunium, and early in his
long life became known for the originality and
independence of his character.   He illustrated

---

[1] Pliny, xxii.   [2] *Ep.* 63.

the doctrines of his school no less by his life than by his teaching. Confining his wants to the barest necessities, living on the roughest fare, clad in the coarsest garments, he was in need of nothing that man could give him, and therefore had no motive for concealing his opinions on life or on the actions of mankind out of any human respect. Seneca, at the summit of his fame and power and wealth, retained the highest admiration and regard for this half-naked champion of poverty and of contempt for the world's goods.

Nature [he says] would seem to have bred him (Demetrius) in our times in order to show that neither could we corrupt him, nor he correct us. He is, though he deny it, a perfectly wise man ; one whose constancy of resolution nothing can shake ; whose un-laboured eloquence following its natural course and intent on its end is little concerned with the choice of words or the modulation of periods, but is exactly suited to the great subjects it treats, and the true expression of a mighty soul. Providence, I am persuaded, has decreed that the man should lead such a life, and has endowed him with such powers of speech, that this age might lack neither an example nor a reproach.[1]

The teaching of Demetrius was that of his school, but confirmed in his instance by an unchanging practice.

The wise man [he taught] must despise whatever is subject to fortune, must raise himself above fear, and learn to attach no value to riches save those that spring from himself, remembering always that there is little to fear from men, and nothing from the goodness of the gods ;

[1] *De Benef.* vii. 8.

he must disdain all those superfluities that torment while they seem to adorn our lives, and understand that death is the source of no evil but the end of many ; consecrating his soul to virtue he must think her way the plainest whithersoever it may lead him ; he must hold himself a social being born for the service of all, and regard the world as a hostel where all men are fellow-sojourners ; he must open his conscience to the gods and live as if all his actions were public.[1]

Among the many great sayings of my friend Demetrius [Seneca writes elsewhere], here is one that I have just heard and that still rings in my ears, ' The man who has never known adversity seems to be un- happiest of all, for he has never been able to test himself.' [2]

Demetrius concealed neither his thoughts nor his dwelling-place, yet he contrived to live without serious molestation under tyrant after tyrant, and died at last in extreme old age in the principate of Domitian. Caligula endeavoured to propitiate him by an enormous present of money, but the philosopher laughingly rejected it, ob- serving afterwards that if the emperor wished to corrupt him he should at least have offered him his whole empire. Later he lived for a time at Corinth, where he made the acquaintance of the thaumaturgist Apollonius of Tyana. Coming to Rome, he became the honoured companion and spiritual adviser of Seneca, Thrasea, and other distinguished men. He was present with Helvidius at Thrasea's death, and it was to him that that high-minded senator addressed his last words.[3] When Nero's gymnasium was completed he made his way into the new building and there

---

[1] *De Benef.* vii. 1.   [2] *De Providentia,* 3.
[3] Tac., *Ann.* xvi. 35:

denounced the custom of bathing, declaring that the bathers only enfeebled and polluted themselves, and that such institutions were a useless expense. ' He was only saved from immediate death, as the penalty of such language, by the fact that Nero was in extra good voice when he sang on that day, which he did in the tavern adjoining the gymnasium, naked, except for a girdle round his waist.'[1] The philosopher was nevertheless charged by Tigellinus with having ruined the bath, and was banished from Rome. After the death of Nero he returned to the city, but, wearing out the patience of Vespasian by the frankness of his criticisms, he was again banished with other philosophers by that emperor.

A third friend of Seneca was Caesonius Maximus. He is only once mentioned in Seneca's letters, but we know from Martial how close was the friendship between the two men. ' This powerful friend of the eloquent Seneca,' writes the poet, ' was almost as dear to him as the beloved Serenus, perhaps even dearer.'[2]

Maximus was a Roman of the governing class who passed through the usual course of honours, ending as *consul suffectus* and proconsul in Sicily under Nero.[3] After Seneca's death Maximus

---

[1] Philostratus, *Apol*. iv. 42.

[2] Martial, vii. 45 :

> ! Facundi Senecae potens amicus,
> Caro proximus, aut prior, Sereno.'

[3] The consuls who gave their name to the year were those appointed on the first of January. These were the *consules ordinarii*, but under the Empire they were accustomed to resign their offices after a few months or even weeks, and *consules suffecti* were appointed to fill their places.

with others of his friends was banished from
Italy without trial. A certain Quintus Ovidius,
to whom Martial afterwards addressed two epigrams, and who, according to that poet, was
to Maximus all that Maximus was to Seneca,
braved the tyrant's resentment by accompanying
him into exile, and earned through this gallant
action such immortality as Martial's verses could
bestow. The letters of Seneca to Maximus were
published and were extant in Martial's time,
but have been lost.[1]

In a letter to Lucilius, Seneca describes a
two days' jaunt made by Maximus and himself.
Their purpose was to try with how many of the
things commonly thought indispensable by a rich
Roman on his travels it was possible, without
real inconvenience, to dispense.

There are many things [he wrote] which we think
necessary, but should not miss if some accident were to
deprive us of them. If, then, we of set purpose went
without them we should not feel their loss. That
lesson I have learnt from my expedition. Starting
with slaves so few that a single waggon could hold
them, and without any luggage that we did not carry
on our persons, I and my friend Maximus have been
enjoying a delightful two days' expedition. I slept
on a mattress spread on the bare ground. One rain-
mantle acted as sheet and one as coverlet. Nothing
unnecessary was served at our meals, which took little
time to prepare. Dried figs were invariable ; and our
tablets were always ready at hand to note impressions.
The figs, when there is bread, serve as a seasoning ; when
there is none, they serve as bread. . . . I drove in a
rustic waggon. The mules just showed they were alive

[1] Tac., *Ann.* xv. 7 ; Martial, vii. 44, 45.

by moving ; the muleteer went barefoot, not because it was summer, but because he had no shoes. I own, however, that I felt some uneasiness at being thought the owner of this conveyance, and the fact that I did so shows that I have not yet succeeded in freeing myself from false shame. Whenever we met some splendid equipage, do what I would I felt embarrassed—a proof that I am not yet steadfastly fixed in the principles I approve and commend, for the man who is ashamed of a humble vehicle will glory in a costly one. I have made little progress. As yet I hardly venture to practise frugality in public ; I still have regard to the opinion of wayfarers.[1]

But the most interesting of Seneca's friends was the Epicurean, Lucilius Junior, to whom the famous letters were addressed, as well as the *Naturales Quaestiones* and the treatise *De Providentia*. Lucilius was an administrator, a philosopher, and a poet. He had known Seneca when they were both young at Pompeii, where he had a house, and where perhaps he was born.

A man [Seneca wrote to him in Sicily] must be dull and insensible indeed, my Lucilius, who forgets his friend until reminded of him by some local association, yet familiar spots do sometimes wake again the sense of bereavement deep hidden in our hearts, not by reviving a perished memory, but by rousing it from slumber. Thus the grief of mourners even when softened by time is renewed by the sight of a familiar slave at the door, or of clothing, or of a house. I cannot describe how I missed you and how fresh seemed the pain of losing you when I arrived in Campania, and especially at Naples and when I saw your Pompeii. I see you with

[1] *Ep.* 87.

extraordinary distinctness, especially as you were when I was quitting you. I see you swallowing your tears and attempting in vain to show no signs of the strong emotion you felt. I seem but yesterday to have lost you. But to those who remember, what may not be called ' yesterday ' ? Only yesterday I sat as a boy under Sotion the philosopher, yesterday I began to plead causes, yesterday I ceased to wish to plead, yesterday I became unable to plead.   Infinite is the swiftness of time.   We see this most clearly when we look back, for it escapes the notice of men intent on the present, so unbroken and continuous is time's headlong flight.   The reason is this. All time past is in the same position ; you may regard it as a whole, it is spread before you and uniform : all things belonging to it are merged in the same abyss, nor, when the whole is brief, can long intervals within it exist. Our actual life is a point, less than a point ; but nature, to make it seem longer, has divided it into parts.   One she has made infancy, another childhood, another youth, another the interval between youth and old age, another old age itself.   How many degrees in so narrow a space ! But a little time ago I was in your company, yet this little time is a considerable part of our life ; on the brevity of which we should constantly meditate.   I used not to think the passage of Time so rapid.   Now its flight seems to me incredibly swift ; whether it is that I see the goal approaching, or whether I have begun to notice and reckon up all I lose.[1]

And in a later letter he relates how the sight of Pompeii again recalled to him Lucilius and his own youth.

Lucilius raised himself from small beginnings by his own industry and talents. During the reigns of Caligula and Claudius he is said to have played a difficult part with honour to him-

[1] *Ep.* 49.

self, to have refused to flatter the reigning
favourites, and to have risked his life through
fidelity to his friends.[1]   Under Nero he became
Procurator of Sicily, and it was from that island
that he corresponded with Seneca.   Seneca warns
him so earnestly against ambition and the danger
of listening to flatterers, that we may fairly conjecture that this warning indicates the presence
of corresponding infirmities in the man to whom
it was addressed.   But he praises his temperance,
modesty, and disinterestedness.

Lucilius from his youth gave much of his
time to liberal studies, and especially to poetry
and philosophy.   While he was in Sicily he wrote,
at the suggestion of Seneca, a poem on Aetna,
which is still extant.[2]   In this poem Lucilius

---

[1] Sen., *Nat. Quaest.* iv. in Praef.   Seneca does not explain the
circumstances to which he alludes.

[2] The authorship has been disputed, especially by Lipsius ;
but the identification seems almost established.   It is probable
that Cornelius Severus, a poet of the Augustan age, whom
Seneca mentions together with Virgil and Ovid as having
treated the subject, and to whom the poem has in consequence
been attributed, like Virgil and Ovid only introduced a description of Aetna into one of his poems ; and in any case he
cannot have been the author of the existing work which contains
words first used in a later generation.   On the other hand, the
coincidences with Seneca are so striking that those who hold
that the poem was written by Severus have been driven to the
hypothesis that Seneca borrowed from it some of his ideas in
the *Naturales Quaestiones.*   Here we have, on the one hand,
a poem written on the subject of Aetna by a philosopher of
the Epicurean school, and from the style and language bearing
the marks of the Neronian age and of the school of Seneca ;
and on the other, a Lucilius Junior who is not only procurator
of Sicily, a poet, and an Epicurean philosopher of the age of
Nero, but one to whom Seneca suggests that he should write
a poem on this very subject.   Such is a summary of part of
the evidence.

K

treats his subject in a scientific and philosophical spirit, discarding, not in silence like Lucan, but with open contempt, all supernatural explanations of the phenomena. The poets, he tells us, vainly imagined the pallid kingdom of Pluto beneath the ashes, the waters of Styx with Cerberus, the giant Tityos spread over seven acres, Tantalus with his eternal thirst foiled by the retreating water, Ixion and the wheel, Minos and his judgments. Not content with this they pry into the manners of the gods, and picture them full of worse than human lusts and passions. But as for me, he continues, ' truth is my only care.' Seneca says the same thing in prose :

Remember [he says to Marcia] that evil exists not for the dead. All those tales of infernal regions are fables invented to terrify us. For the dead there is neither darkness nor prison, nor rivers of fire, nor Lethe, nor tribunals, nor accused. In that free state there are no fresh tyrants. These things are the fond imaginations of poets who delude us into empty fears. Death is alike the reward and the end of all pain ; beyond it our sufferings cannot extend ; it replaces us in that state of perfect tranquillity which was ours before we were born. If we pity the dead, we should pity those unborn.

And again, in the treatise *De Vita Beata* he speaks of the folly of poets who impute every vice to Jupiter—making him a parricide, a usurper, and a seducer. Their motive must be, he says, to relieve men by such examples from any sense of guilt in their own actions.[1]

[1] *Aetna*, 72–89 ; Seneca, *Cons. ad Marc.* 19 ; *De Vita Beata*, 26.

For Seneca philosophy was divided into two branches, the one concerned with human and the other with divine matters. The former is what we should now call moral philosophy or ethics ; the latter natural science. For the purely speculative part of philosophy, for all that had no bearing either upon the conduct of human life or upon the order of nature, he felt not only indifference but an impatient contempt. Lucilius, on the other hand, was much more attracted by metaphysics. He enjoyed the logical puzzles, paradoxes, and distinctions of the schools, and was constantly endeavouring in his letters to entice Seneca into abstract discussions. Again, in the matter of style, to which Lucilius attached a high importance, Seneca is constantly impressing upon him the danger of paying too much attention to words. ' *Oratio vultus animi est,*' he says. ' Speech is the countenance of the soul ; if it is over-polished and coloured and, so to speak, manipulated, one infers that the soul also is unsound and feeble.' Constantly he returns to these topics, and dwells on the waste of time involved in idle exercises of ingenuity.

How do they help me ? [he asks]. Do they make me braver, more just, more temperate ? I have no leisure for such exercises ; I still need a doctor. Why teach me this useless science ? You promise great things ; you give me small ones. You told me I should be fearless when swords were glancing around me, when the dagger's point was at my throat ; you said I should be without concern in fire or shipwreck. Teach me to despise pleasure and glory ; when I have learnt that, we may proceed to the solution of riddles, to nice distinctions, to the elucidation of obscurities ; for the present let us keep to the essential.[1]

To understand Seneca's reiterated insistence in these letters on the vital necessity of a mental discipline which should brace the mind against all that might befall, and prepare a man to face death at any moment at the hands of a tyrant, we must remember that they were written at a time when these trials were becoming increasingly possible for every man of mark. Philosophy, he is always saying, is concerned with action, not with words ; and the test of proficiency is the concordance of practice with theory. It teaches us to distinguish realities from appearances. Death, for instance, may come through a tyrant or a fever, pain through disease or an executioner ; such differences cannot change their nature, they are still but death and pain. Yet we fear them far more in the one case than in the other, for it is the pomp and circumstance of things and not the things themselves that form the subjects of our fear.[2] ' Remember,' he tells him, ' that there is nothing admirable in man except his soul, to which when great all other things are small.'[3] Wisdom consists in constancy of will—a constancy unalter-

---

[1] *Ep.* 109. In this long controversy between the rhetoricians and philosophers, between ' the artists of the pure form of speech and the investigators of the inmost nature of things,' Seneca, in direct opposition to his father's view, was the protagonist of the philosophers. See Friedländer, iii. 3.

[2] ' Efficientia non effectum spectat timor.'

[3] ' Cogita in te, praeter animum, nihil esse mirabile : cui magno nihil magnum est ' (*Ep.* 8).

able by external circumstances. It is thus that
the service of philosophy becomes the only true
freedom. This constancy can only be acquired
by continual attention to realities—the spinning
of syllogisms and the ravelling and unravelling
of academical knots are nothing to the purpose.
It is the first sign of a weak and untrained mind
to dread the unexperienced. To banish this dread
should be the chief end of our endeavours. We
shall find our medicine pleasant to the taste, for
it is one that pleases while it heals.

A happy life [he says] is founded in a freedom from
concern and an abiding tranquillity. These are the gifts
of greatness of soul, and of a steady persistence in what
has been well resolved. We may reach this goal if
we behold truth as a whole, if in all we do we preserve
order, moderation, fitness, and a will guiltless and kindly,
looking to Reason for guidance and never departing
from her precepts, which are alike lovable and wondrous.
. . . Let the man who finds his chief good in tastes
and colours and sounds renounce the fellowship of the
most glorious of living beings second only to the gods;
and join dumb animals rejoicing in their pasture. . . .
No man is free who is the slave of his body. For
not only does his anxiety on its behalf throw him into
the power of all those who can injure it, but it is itself
a surly and exacting commander. The free spirit
sometimes quits it with calm indifference, sometimes
springs from it with a generous ardour, and in either
case cares as little for its future destiny as we do for
that of the bristles of our beards after shaving.[1]

Though the main object of Seneca's counsels
was to prepare his friend to meet with forti-

[1] *Ep. 92.*

tude whatever fate might have in store for
him, he does not neglect the humbler warnings
of prudence. He advises him to live as retired
a life as possible, to avoid singularity, to occupy
himself as little as possible with politics while
avoiding a conspicuous withdrawal from them,
for this too excites suspicion, and to be cautious
with whom he conversed.

For your greater security [he writes] I would have you
observe certain precautions, which you must take from
me as though I were prescribing rules for the preserva-
tion of your health when living in your Ardeatine villa.
Reflect what are the motives which incite a man to
the destruction of another : you will find them to be
hope, envy, hatred, fear, or contempt.

He proceeds to give admirable advice as to
how to avoid exciting these emotions in the
minds of others; but ends by saying that, after
all, every man's best security is his innocence,
and that the guilty, though they sometimes
chance to escape, can never feel sure of doing so.
The man is punished who expects punishment ;
and whoever deserves it expects it. Thus the
imprudent always suffer the penalty of their follies
and crimes. But if all these precautions are
taken, can I guarantee your safety ? I can no
more promise you that, replies Seneca, than I can
promise perpetual health to a man who takes due
care of himself.[1] Roman senators during the last
half of Nero's principate lived under a sword of
Damocles comparable to that which threatened
French aristocrats during the Reign of Terror.

[1] *Ep.* 14.

' *Palpitantibus praecordiis vivitur.*' The mission of
Seneca was to give courage to the despairing, to
teach them to meet death with fortitude, and to
convince them that no man need be a slave, since
the liberty to die could not be taken from him.
Thus the great refuge from tyranny was self-
destruction, the right to which he asserts time
and again with terrible earnestness. 'There are
professors of wisdom,' he writes, 'to whom it is
anathema to offer violence to our own persons or
cut short our own lives. We must wait till Nature
releases us. Those who say this do not see that
they are barring the way to liberty. The eternal
law contains nothing better than this, that it has
given us only one entrance into life but many
exits.' 'No one is justified in complaining of life,
for no one is obliged to live. Are you content?
Then live. Not content? You may return whence
you came.'[1] And later in the same letter, 'The way
to that great liberty is opened with a bodkin: our
safety is contained in a prick.'[2] And again in the
De Ira: 'Wherever you cast your eyes you
will find the end of your ills. Do you see that
precipice? It is the descent to liberty. That sea?
that river? that well? Beneath their waters liberty
lies concealed. Do you see that little misshapen
tree? There hangs liberty.'[3]

---

[1] *Ep.* 68: 'Hoc est unum, cur de vita non possumus queri;
neminem tenet. . . . Placet? vive. Non placet? licet eo reverti
unde venisti.'

[2] 'Scalpello aperitur ad illam magnam libertatem via: et
puncto securitas constat.' Cp. *Hamlet*, 'When he himself may
his quietus make with a bare bodkin.'

[3] *De Ira*, ii. 15.

CHAPTER XI

SENECA was greatly interested in an expedition
round Sicily made by Lucilius, and the letter in
which he speaks of it may be given in full, not
only as an illustration of his inquiring and speculative mind, but because in it he makes the first
suggestion of the poem on Aetna :

I am waiting for your letters to hear what new dis-
coveries you have made in sailing round Sicily, and
especially what fuller information you can give me
about Charybdis. For I know very well that Scylla
is a rock and not very formidable to navigators, but I
am anxious to hear from you whether Charybdis answers
to her reputation in story. If you happen to have
observed it (and it is worthy of observation), tell me
whether the whirlpools appear when the wind is in one
quarter only, or if that sea is afflicted with them in
every kind of weather ; and also if it is true that anything drawn into that vortex is carried many miles
under water and only reappears near the coast of Tauro-
menium. After you have written fully to me of all this,
I shall venture to commission you further, for my sake,
to ascend Aetna, which is said to have been formerly
seen by navigators from a greater distance than now,
whence the inference is drawn that it is consuming

away and gradually subsiding.   But the cause may rather
be that the fire has died away and bursts forth with
less force and magnitude than formerly, the smoke also
becoming more sluggish for the same reason.   Neither
of these theories is incredible ; the one that the
mountain by daily consumption is becoming less, the
other that the fire does not remain the same—the fire
that does not spring from the mountain itself but boils
up from some underground pit where it is generated
and fed from below, the mountain itself yielding it not
aliment but a passage.   There is a well-known district
in Lycia, called Hephaestion by the inhabitants, where
the soil is perforated in several places, and a perfectly
harmless fire runs round it which does no injury to
the plants.   So the country is fertile and grassy, nothing
is scorched by the flames, which glimmer but faintly
and have no force.   But let us reserve these things
for another time, and then when you write to me on
the subject I shall also ask how far the snows, which
even summer cannot melt, much less the volcanic fires,
are distant from the crater's mouth.   And you have no
right to impute this trouble to me, for if no one had
commissioned you to do so you suffer from a certain
malady which would not have allowed you to rest till
you had described Aetna in a poem and approached this
ground sacred for all poets.   That Virgil had already
done full justice to this subject did not prevent Ovid
from handling it ; nor did both of them together deter
Severus Cornelius.   So happy a material does this place
afford to all, that those who have gone before appear
to me not to have anticipated all that can be said, but
to have opened the way.   It makes a great difference
whether your subject has been exhausted or only treated ;
in the latter case it grows as time goes on, and the invention of former writers is no obstacle to that of their
successors.   Moreover, the latter are placed in the best
position.   They find words ready for use, and by arrang-
ing these differently can give them a new appearance ;
nor do they steal them as if they belonged to others,

for they are public property. Lawyers deny that any public property can be appropriated by prescription. I am mistaken in you if Aetna does not whet your appetite. Already you are wishing to write something great and equal to the work of your predecessors—equal, I say, for your modesty does not allow you to hope for more ; a modesty so great that I think you would rather withhold something from the full force of your genius than run the risk of surpassing them, so high is your reverence for the elder poets. Wisdom has this good point among the rest, that no one can be surpassed therein by another except during the ascent. When you reach the summit all are equal, there is no room for an increase, a halt is made. Can the sun add aught to his greatness ? Can the moon wax further than she is wont ? The seas do not increase ; the universe preserves the same habit and measure. Whatever has completed its natural magnitude cannot gain in stature. Wise men, in so far as wise, are equal and on a level. Each of them may have his own proper gifts : one will be more easy of access, another readier, another more fluent, another more eloquent ; that wisdom of which we are speaking, that only source of happiness, will be equal in all. Whether your Aetna can sink down and fall in upon itself, or whether the constant action of the fire can draw down this lofty summit, so conspicuous over a wide expanse of sea, I know not ; neither flame nor crumbling away can lower the height of virtue. This is the one majesty that can never be degraded ; it can be neither extended nor reduced. Its magnitude is fixed, like that of the heavenly bodies. To her let us endeavour to raise ourselves : much is already done, or rather, to confess the truth, not much. For it is not goodness to be better than the worst. Who boasts of eyes that shrink from daylight ? for which the sun shines through a mist ? Though he may be satisfied to have escaped from total darkness, he does not yet enjoy the full light of day. Then will our soul have cause for rejoicing when escaping from the darkness in which it was involved, it sees no longer dimly and uncertainly, but admits the perfect light ; when it is restored to its heavenly home and has recovered the place to which it was born. Our soul's origin calls it heavenward. It will gain heaven even before it is loosed from these bonds if it fling away its faults and emerge unstained and untrammelled into the contemplation of the divine mysteries. This is what we should do, my dearest Lucilius ; toward this end should we strain with our whole strength, though few know what we do, and none see us. Glory is the shadow of virtue ; it will accompany even those who shun it. ' But just as a shadow sometimes goes before and sometimes follows after, so glory is sometimes before us and offers itself to the view, but at other times holds back until envy has passed away, when it appears the greater for having come late. How long Democritus seemed a madman ! Fame scarce welcomed Socrates. How long was Cato ignored by the State ! It rejected him, and only understood when it had lost him. Had Rutilius never suffered wrong his innocence and virtue would have remained hidden ; he became famous through the violence done to him. Did he not thank his fortune and embrace his exile ? I speak of those whom Fortune by persecution has rendered illustrious in their lifetime ; how many are those whose accomplishments have become known only after their death ! how many whom Fame has not received but dragged out ! You see how greatly not merely the learned, but this whole throng of the unlearned, admire Epicurus. He was quite unknown at Athens itself, where he lived in obscurity. Many years after the death of his friend Metrodorus, speaking in one of his letters with grateful recollection of their friendship, he ends with this—that among so many advantages it was of no disservice to Metrodorus and himself that they lived in that famous country of Greece, not only unknown, but almost unheard. Did he on this account remain undiscovered after he had ceased to exist ? Did not his opinions then shine forth ? Metrodorus also confesses in one of his letters that Epicurus and himself were less audible than they should have been, but foretold that they would have a great and established name among those who were willing to follow in their footsteps. No virtue remains concealed; to have lain concealed is no loss. The day will come which will reveal what is hidden and suppressed by the malignity of the age. The man who thinks only of his own generation is born for few. Many thousands of years, many thousands of peoples, will come after: look to them. Even if all your contemporaries are silent through envy, there will come those who will judge you without favour or prejudice. If Fame can offer any reward to virtue, neither will this be lost. The verdict of posterity, indeed, will be nothing to us; yet posterity will honour us and resort to us though we perceive it not. Virtue will requite us whether alive or dead, if only we follow her in good faith, if we adorn not ourselves with the false and meretricious, but remain the same whether we have to act in a conspicuous position and after due warning; or suddenly and unprepared. Simulation profits nothing. A false exterior adopted for appearance' sake imposes superficially upon a few; truth is always the same in all her parts. There is no solidity in the things that deceive. A lie is thin; if you look closely you can see through it.[1]

Seneca was immensely rich. His gardens (' *Senecae praedivitis hortos* '[2]), his villas, his furniture were renowned; and although he was completely free from the grosser forms of self-indulgence and was personally simple to the point of austerity in his manner of life, these riches and the elegance of his surroundings laid him open to a charge of inconsistency between his theory and his practice, which was pressed home by his enemies during his lifetime, and has never ceased to be repeated

---

[1] *Ep.* 79.　　　　[2] Juv. ix.

by later critics. But to suppose that Seneca thought riches an evil in themselves—as the first Christians, who were his contemporaries and whose teaching resembles his on many other points, really did think—is to misunderstand his whole doctrine. Things in themselves, according to the Stoics, are neither good nor evil, but only the use we make of them and the manner in which we regard and handle them. They are the material, not the substance, of good and evil. A wise man may possess riches so long as he regards himself merely as Fortune's banker, and is ready to yield them up at her demand with as little regret as a banker pays out the deposits of his clients. The danger is lest the rich man should confound his shirt with his skin and regard his possessions as part of himself. If he does not do this he may without inconsistency prefer riches to poverty, just as he may deny that exile is an evil, and yet if it be in his power spend his life in his native land, or as he may think a short life as desirable as a long, and yet may live to a tranquil old age. The reason, indeed, for thinking lightly of such things is not that we may rid ourselves of them, but that we may enjoy them without anxiety. The difference between you and me, wrote Seneca to his critics, is that my riches belong to me ; you to your riches.

In the treatise *De Vita Beata*, addressed to his brother Gallio, Seneca stated with uncompromising frankness and force—impossible, one would think, to a disingenuous man—the charges brought against him on this head, and gave his answer.

The following extracts will enable the reader to form his own judgment on accusation and defence. The genuine humility of the man—rare indeed among Romans—his objective outlook and his mental detachment, are nowhere more conspicuous.

If, then, one of these barking critics of philosophy says to me : ' Why are your words so much stronger than your deeds ? How is it that you talk submissively to superiors ; and consider money a necessary means to your ends, and are affected by its loss ? Why do you weep when you hear of the loss of a wife or a friend ? Why are you careful of your reputation and vexed by slander ? Why that elaborate adornment of your country-seats so far beyond the needs of nature ? Why are your banquets not restricted to the limits of your rule ? Why this beautiful furniture, this wine older than yourself, these trees that yield nothing but shade ? Why does your wife wear in her ears the fortune of a rich family ? Why are your attendants clothed in precious raiment ? Why does the service at your house amount to a fine art, the plate arranged with the utmost skill and attention, the chief carver himself an artist ? ' You may add if you please : ' Why do you possess estates across the sea ? Why have you slaves whose names you know not ?—are you so forgetful that you cannot remember the few there are, or are you so unthrifty as to have more than you can remember ? ' I will help you to abase me anon and suggest for your use fresh objections which have escaped your attention : now hear my reply. ' I am not a wise man, and, so please your malice, I never shall be. I therefore do not claim to be equal with the best, but only better than the worst. Enough for me if every day I make some little progress, and can clearly see and denounce my own errors. I am not cured ; I never shall be cured. I contrive palliations rather than remedies for my malady ; and am content if its attacks become gradually rarer.

Compared to your pace, however, I am a tolerable runner. In what I am going to say I speak not for myself; for I am sunk in every kind of fault, but for one who has made progress. This charge of inconsistency was brought by the malignant enemies of all virtue against Plato, against Epicurus, against Zeno. It is of virtue, not of myself, that I speak; I make war upon vices, my own before all others. When I can, may I live as I ought. Your poisonous malice, the gall with which in sprinkling others you destroy yourselves, shall never affright me from communion with the best, or prevent me from celebrating—not the life which I lead, but the life which I know should be led—or from adoring virtue and following her footsteps at however vast a distance, even on my hands and knees. . . . Philosophers, it is said, do not practise what they preach. But they practise much of what they preach and finely conceive. If, indeed, their lives were on a level with their doctrines, what could equal their felicity? In the meantime good words and a breast stocked with good thoughts are not to be despised. So excellent a form of study, though it fail of its full effect, in itself deserves to be had in honour. What wonder that few should reach so difficult a summit? Yet we ought to respect the climbers, even if they slip; for great is their attempt. The man is generous who, regarding not his own individual strength but that of the nature proper to man, conceives in his mind and endeavours to carry out an ideal so high that in practice it lies beyond the reach even of the loftiest of the human race. Such a man has thus resolved within himself: ' I will meet death as calmly as I hear of it: my soul supporting my body, there is no labour that I will not undergo. Riches, whether present or absent, I will equally despise; neither the sadder if I have them not, nor elated if they shine in my possession. I shall consider all land as if it were mine; my own land as if it belonged to all. I shall live as knowing that I am born for others; and for this I shall give thanks to Nature. For how could she better have consulted my interests? She gave me to all men ; but she has given all men to me. That which I have I shall neither meanly hoard nor foolishly squander. None of my possessions will seem to me more truly my own than what I have well bestowed ; benefits I shall reckon neither by number nor by weight, but by the worth of the recipient. I shall never count the cost of what I give to merit. Opinion shall never, and conscience always, guide my actions. . . . I will be pleasant to my friends, mild and placable to my enemies, I will forgive before my forgiveness is asked, I will satisfy all honest petitions. I shall know that the world is my country with the gods as its rulers, and these I shall regard as the judges of all I do and all I say. And so whenever Nature takes once more my spirit to herself, or when my reason releases it, I shall go hence bearing witness that I have loved a good conscience and a good manner of life, and that none through me have suffered loss of liberty, myself least of all.' [1]

Such was the apologia of Seneca, and we cannot doubt that it was sincere. His personal habits were simple to the verge of austerity ; the choice wine that he gave to his guests he did not himself touch ; he was distinguished as a generous friend to honest poverty, especially among men of letters ; nothing is recorded by historians of his five years of power to lead us to question the truth of his boast, that by his means no man had been unjustly deprived of liberty.

But there was another consideration relating to the source of his wealth which he could not directly advance, but which he suggested in several other passages in his books. Without mortal offence to the emperor he could not have refused his gifts. In his treatise 'On Benefits'

[1] *De Vita Beata*, 17, 20.

he lays down the rule that we should not receive favours except from those on whom, were
the circumstances altered, we would confer them.
It is a burden to incur obligation to those whom
we can neither love nor respect.   Thereupon the
question is raised whether if a brutal and passionate
tyrant, who will hold himself insulted by a refusal,
offers us a present we are bound to refuse it.
The king has the soul, let us say, of a robber or
pirate and is unworthy that we should accept
his bounty.   The answer made is that when we
are free to choose we must take nothing from
the unworthy ; but that in the case supposed we
are not accepting but obeying,[1] and again :

To refuse a gift is to incense against ourselves an
insolent monarch, who would have all that comes from
his hands valued at a high rate.   It matters not whether
you are unwilling to give to a king or to receive from
him, the offence is equal in either case, or rather even
graver in the latter, since to the proud it is more bitter
to be disdained than not to be feared.[2]

In another passage of the same work he dis-
cusses the question whether gratitude is due to
tyrants, and whether their favours should be returned, and answers affirmatively with respect to
all cases where this is consistent with the public
weal.   If, he says, he had had the misfortune to
be obliged by one who subsequently became the
most infamous of tyrants, who found a pleasure
in shedding human blood and breaking all the
rights and laws of human society, then he would
feel all bonds dissolved between them, because

[1] *De Benef.* ii. 18.   [2] *Ibid.*, v. 6.

L

the duty he owed to humanity must always take precedence of an obligation to a single individual.

But [he adds] although this is so, and although from the time when by violating every human right and so making it impossible for himself to be wronged by any man, he has made me free to do what I will against him, yet I shall still reckon myself bound to discharge my debt so far as may stand with my public duty. I must not add to his power for evil ; I must not increase his destructive forces or confirm those he has. But if without injury to the commonwealth I may return his kindness, I will do so. I would save his infant son from death, for that could not injure the victims of his cruelty ; but I would not contribute a penny to the support of his mercenaries. If he hanker after marbles and fine raiment, that can do no mischief to any man, and I will help him to them ; soldiers and arms I will not supply. If he entreat me as a great kindness to send him comedians and women, and other such delights which may temper his brutality, I will find them for him willingly. Though I will not supply him with triremes and ships of war, he shall have luxuriously fitted boats of pleasure for his amusement. But if I despair altogether of his amendment, the same hand shall at one blow discharge my debt to him and confer a benefit on all mankind, for to such a nature death is a remedy, and to speed his departure the one kindness I can do him.[1]

These words were written after Seneca's retirement and shortly before the outbreak of the conspiracy of Piso, with the aims of which, whether he knew of it or not, he must unquestionably have sympathised. By that time Nero had sunk into

[1] *De Benef.* vii. 20.

an abyss of infamy from which it was evident
that death alone could rescue him.

That Seneca made a good and generous use
of his riches, we have not only his own testimony
but that of Juvenal and Martial. And first as
to his own. In the *De Vita Beata*, after explaining that a philosopher may legitimately be rich,
provided that his riches are honourably acquired,
taken from no man, earned at the expense of
no man's sufferings, stained with no blood, and
spent as honourably as they were gained, he adds
that they should not be rejected, unless either
they are thought by their possessor to be useless,
or unless he confesses that he does not know
how to use them. This brings him to a description of their proper employment, and he proceeds
thus :

He will give either to the good, or to those whom he
can make good. He will take the greatest trouble to
discover the worthiest and give to them, as one who
remembers that he must account not only for what he has
received but for what he has spent. He will give for good
and adequate reasons, since an ill-bestowed gift must be
counted as a bad form of wastefulness. His purse will be
open indeed, but have no holes in it ; much will come
from it, but nothing fall. It is a mistake to suppose that
bounty is an easy art. If it is thoughtfully given, if
there is no promiscuous squandering, it is on the contrary
most difficult. I oblige one man, I discharge my obligations to another, I come to the aid of a third, I take
pity on a fourth. I find one whose poverty binds him
to occupations unworthy of his abilities—I release
him from that poverty. To some, even though they
are in need, I will not give, because, whatever I give,
they will always be in need ; to others I will offer aid

though they have not asked it ; on others, again, I
will press it though they refuse. I cannot be careless
in this matter ; I never invest with more care than in
stock of this nature. Do you expect interest, then ?
I am asked. Well, at least, I do not wish to throw my
investment away. I wish so to place my donation that
though I must never seek a return, yet I may believe
a return to be possible. It should resemble a buried
treasure which you do not disinter unless it be necessary.
What an opportunity for kindness may not a rich man
find in his own household—for why should our liberality
be confined to the free ? Nature bids us do good unto
all men, whether free legally, or virtually by our consent :
wherever there is a man, there is room for kindness.[1]

Such were Seneca's views, instinct with his
customary good sense and moderation, on the
subject of almsgiving and the use of money.
They have a modern ring, and would have qualified
him in the island of Britain eighteen hundred years
later for high office in the Charity Organisation
Society. We have some evidence that, in this
instance at least, his practice was on a level with
his precepts.

No one [wrote Juvenal, some twenty years after-
wards] now expects to receive what Seneca used to
send to very humble friends, or what the good Piso
or Cotta used to give ; for in those days a bountiful
disposition was thought to add lustre to honours and
titles.[2]

And Martial, whose Spanish origin may have
recommended him to Seneca, in the same vein re-
grets in two of his epigrams the spacious days of
Piso and Seneca and Memmius, whom he prefers

---

[1] *De Vita Beata*, 24.   [2] Juv. v. 108.

to the most liberal patrons of his own time.[1]
Three other of Martial's epigrams are addressed
to Lucan's widow Polla, so that it is clear that his
friendship with Seneca's family did not end with
the philosopher's death.[2]

[1] Martial, iv. 40 ; xii. 36.   [2] *Ibid.*, vii. 21, 22, 23.

CHAPTER XII

THE CONSPIRACY OF PISO AND THE DEATH OF SENECA, A.D. 64–65

THE last public office held by Seneca was that of *consul suffectus*, which he shared with Trebellius Maximus. During their consulship a *senatus consultum* was passed to protect executors or trustees, who by a legal fiction were technically the sole heirs of the estates which they administered, from liabilities attaching to such estates, on the principle that no man ought to suffer on account of a trust which he has faithfully discharged.[1] Trebellius was afterwards governor of Britain, where his inactivity and want of military experience made him unpopular with the army. The date of this consulship is generally assigned to the year 62, on the insufficient ground that Tacitus makes mention of a decree passed

---

[1] *Ins. Tit.* 23 (4): 'Neronis quidem temporibus, Trebellio Maximo et Annaeo Seneca coss. senatus-consultum factum est, quo cautum est, ut, si haereditas ex fidei-commissi causa restituta sit, actiones, quae jure civili haeredi et in haeredem competerent, ei et in eum darentur, cui ex fidei-commisso restituta esset haereditas. Post quod senatus-consultum, praetor utiles actiones ei et in eum qui recepit haereditatem, quasi haeredi et in haeredem, dare coepit.'

by the Senate in that year for the restraint of fictitious adoptions.[1]

The year 64, though a year of peace, was one of calamity for Rome. From the time when Tigellinus had succeeded to the power and influence of Seneca and Burrhus, the progress of Nero in the path of infamy had become ever more rapid. Early in this year he sang on the stage of the theatre at Naples, choosing that city for his first public appearance because its population was Greek. Thence he designed to go to Greece, the home of the arts, and compete for prizes at the historical festivals; but abandoned that project for the time. He then returned to Rome and made preparations for a visit to Egypt; but, to the great joy of the populace, who thought that his presence in Rome secured their supply of amusements and provisions, he changed his mind as to this also and remained in the city. Charmed with this evidence of the popularity he always coveted, and inferring that it was more easily and more agreeably gained by the methods of Tigellinus than by those recommended by Seneca, he thereupon plunged into the wildest excesses of luxury, extravagance, and open debauchery. He entertained the citizens at gorgeous banquets in public places,

[1] It seems unlikely that Seneca should have been named consul by the emperor in the year of the death of Burrhus and his own partial disgrace. On the other hand, we know that Nero refused to accept his resignation, and may at that time have designated him consul as a mark of continued confidence. Moreover Trebellius, who was governor of Britain at the time of Nero's death, would probably have received this appointment not very long after holding the consulship.

seemed to regard, in Tacitus' phrase, the whole city as his house, and prostituted the noblest Romans to the pleasures of the mob.

There followed the great fire, in the course of which the greater part of Rome was burnt to the ground. Nero, who was reported to have watched the flames from the tower of Maecenas with aesthetic delight, while he chanted in costume a poem of his own composition on the destruction of Troy, was accused of having himself contrived the fire. Incendiaries were seen in the confusion rushing about with torches in their hands, stopping attempts to extinguish the fire, and crying out that they had authority for what they were doing. These were probably robbers, but they were widely believed to be emissaries of the emperor. Nero, alarmed at the loss of his darling popularity, was roused to unwonted efforts. He threw open his gardens and the Campus Martius to the homeless multitude, and ran up hastily built shelters for their reception ; he imported necessaries from Ostia and the neighbouring towns ; he supplied the people with food at the lowest prices. Finally, he sought to divert suspicion from himself by accusing the new and unpopular sect of Christians of the crime, and after having by torture extracted confessions from some among them, large numbers were arrested on their information and put to horrible deaths. He illuminated his gardens at night with the burning bodies of these victims, and in the habit of a charioteer mingled with the throng at the circus games, where the Christian martyrs, clad in the skins of wild beasts, were torn to pieces by his hounds.

Whether or not Nero was concerned in the burning of Rome, the catastrophe allowed him to satisfy his passion for the grandiose in the rebuilding of Rome, and especially of his own palace, on a magnificent scale. The old city with its tall houses and narrow winding streets was gone, and broad regular thoroughfares with houses of moderate height, built of stone and fronted by colonnades, were laid out in its place. At the same time a fire-brigade and an improved water-supply were organised. For the erection of his own ' Golden House,' with its gardens and lakes, its woods and solitudes, its open spaces and prospects, a large area was reserved, and even the Romans of that day, accustomed as they were to every form of idle display, were amazed at its superb extravagance.

This reckless prodigality, coinciding as it did with the great destruction of wealth due to the fire, was followed by the inevitable consequences. The treasury was exhausted, and could only be refilled by injustice and oppression. Italy, says Tacitus, was devastated, the provinces ruined. The gods themselves did not escape, for the temples were despoiled of their treasures and their images, and ancient historical memorials ruthlessly destroyed in both Italy and Greece. Seneca, who, though he had lost all influence, had never been allowed entirely to break his connection with the government, protested against these proceedings, and, when his protests were disregarded, made a last effort to obtain permission to withdraw into some distant retreat. When this was refused, he made his health a pretext for not quitting his bed-chamber, and is said to have guarded himself against Nero's attempts to poison him by reducing his diet to water and the simplest food, the source of which he could control. This is the last notice we have of his intervention in public affairs.

The following year (65), the last of Seneca's life, was marked by the great conspiracy of Piso and the ruthless proscription of senators and others that followed its discovery. Piso, the head of the ancient and illustrious Calpurnian family, had been favoured alike by nature and by fortune, and was perhaps the most popular man in Rome. With a handsome countenance and a graceful person he showed courtesy to all, and indulged the love of magnificence which he combined with literary tastes in a profusion which conciliated the affections and gained the admiration of a pleasure-loving age. He was a generous patron of men of letters, and was bracketed with his friend Seneca in regretful reminiscence by the Flavian poets. He was, moreover, famed for his eloquence, which he had employed in pleading the cause of citizens in the Forum. With all these advantages Piso was too indolent and easy-going to make a good chief of an enterprise that required energy, active ambition, and resolution to bring it to a successful issue.

The object of the conspiracy was the death of Nero and the transfer of the Empire to Piso.

The conspirators were many in number, and for the most part of senatorial or equestrian rank. They included the consul designate Plautius Lateranus ; Lucan, the poet who, forbidden by Nero to publish or recite his poetry, had already avenged himself in secret by the invective against the tyranny of the Caesars contained in the later books of the *Pharsalia* ; Subrius Flavius, a tribune of the praetorian guard ; Senecio, who had been an intimate friend of Nero's ; and Fenius Rufus, the colleague of Tigellinus in his praetorian command. Various schemes, dictated by their respective temperaments, were suggested by one or other of the plotters. Some were for boldly attacking the emperor while he was singing on the public stage, trusting for success to the disgust so widely felt for these performances ; but the desire for impunity, ' ever adverse to great enterprises,' led others to prefer a scheme for setting fire to the palace, when Nero might be slain in the midst of the ensuing confusion. While the conspirators were discussing these proposals and disputing with one another, the indiscretion of a woman named Epicharis nearly led to the discovery of the plot. Volusius Proculus, who had been among those employed by Nero in the murder of his mother, was a naval officer of the fleet at Misenum in high command. Dissatisfied with the manner in which his guilty services had been rewarded, he complained of his wrongs to Epicharis, and spoke of revenge. This woman, who was in the secret of the plot, was induced by his words to hope that she might obtain for her friends this important recruit, and so, without betraying the names of the conspirators, sufficiently indicated what was afoot to lead him to report to the emperor what he had heard. Epicharis was summoned to Rome and confronted with the informer who, however, found it impossible to confute her resolute denials. Nero's suspicions had nevertheless been aroused, and Epicharis was detained in custody.

This alarm determined the conspirators to hasten their attempt. Nero was about to be Piso's guest in his villa at Baiae, and the opportunity seemed to many of them an excellent one for carrying out their designs. But Piso refused to violate, after the manner of Macbeth, the laws of hospitality. ' Better,' he said, ' that the deed should be done in the city, in that detested house founded on the spoils of citizens. What was done for the sake of the republic should be done openly.' At last they resolved to execute their plot at the Circus' games, where Nero was more accessible than at other times. Lateranus, on pretence of a petition, was to fall at the knees of the emperor and, seizing them, to overturn him, when the other conspirators would attack him with their daggers. Piso, who was to await events at the Temple of Ceres, was then to be summoned to the camp by Fenius the prefect and by others, and proclaimed emperor. The first blow was to be struck by Flavius Scevinus, a conspirator of senatorial rank, who had consecrated to this end a dagger in the Temple of Safety, and now withdrew it for its work.

To the imprudence of Scevinus the discovery

of the conspiracy was due. On the day before that fixed upon for the execution of the plot, after a long conference with his fellow-conspirator Natalis, he returned home, signed his will, and complaining of the rustiness of the dagger which he had withdrawn from the temple, ordered his freedman Milichus to sharpen it. There followed a dinner of unwonted splendour and numerously attended, when it was evident to all that the host had something on his mind, and the gaiety which he affected appeared forced and unnatural. Afterwards he emancipated his favourite slaves, and gave presents of money to others ; and, lastly, he bade Milichus prepare bandages for wounds, and all that was necessary for stopping the flow of blood. All these circumstances roused the suspicions of Milichus. The hope of reward with the fear lest his treachery might be anticipated by the inferences of some other observer from the same tokens, in which case his fidelity would be of no service to his master and dangerous to himself, overcame his sense of obligation to the patron to whom he owed his freedom, and led him early the next morning to report his suspicions to the emperor. Scevinus was seized and brought to the palace. There he answered the charges with boldness, denying some of the acts imputed to him, and explaining others with such plausibility that the charge would have broken down had not Milichus recalled the conference with Natalis and suggested that the latter should be arrested and examined as to its subject. This was done, and Natalis and

Scevinus, being separately examined and giving inconsistent accounts of their conversation, were flung into irons and, succumbing to the threat of torture, made both of them a full confession, each doubtless under the impression that the other had first confessed. Natalis was the first to name Piso, and then with the view, according to Tacitus, of giving pleasure to Nero, he related that he had visited Seneca on Piso's behalf to complain of the cessation of their intercourse. Seneca, he said, had excused himself on the ground that frequent conversations and meetings would conduce to the interests of neither, but had added that his own welfare depended on Piso's safety. Lucan and others were incriminated by Scevinus. Lucan, after long denials, was led to confess by a promise of pardon, but admirers of his poetry may hope that the report that, in order to conciliate the sympathy of a matricide emperor, he had the unspeakable baseness to accuse his mother, Atilia, of complicity was an invention of his enemies.

Nero now bethought himself of Epicharis, who had been detained in custody on the information of Proculus. Tigellinus caused this woman to be questioned under torture; but the most exquisite inventions of his exasperated cruelty could not wring from her a single name, and while on the second day, unable to walk, she was being supported to the torture-chamber, she contrived by strangling herself to thwart the further efforts of her persecutors. Her constancy was in striking contrast to the weakness of her distinguished confederates, whose courage had

been broken by the very sight of instruments
of torture.

The friends of Piso urged him at this juncture
to repair to the camp and appeal to soldiers and
populace. As things were, they said, nothing
worse could happen to him if he failed than if
he submitted, while Nero with his degenerate
following were easily to be overcome. But the
indolent and indifferent Piso was destitute of
the imagination that might have brought such
an attempt to a successful issue. Without awaiting the band of soldiers sent by the emperor
to arrest him—a band chosen from among the
most recent recruits, since the fidelity of the
veterans in such an employment was suspect—
he opened his veins and died, having first drawn
up a will wherein in terms of fulsome adulation
he made a large legacy to the emperor, in the
hope of thereby securing a peaceful succession
to the rest of his estate for the beautiful wife
whom he had stolen from a friend. There followed a great proscription of conspirators real
or alleged, conducted with great cruelty by
Tigellinus, actively assisted by his colleague,
Fenius Rufus, who hoped by the zeal with which
he prosecuted his late accomplices to clear himself from all suspicion of a share in their guilt.

Whether or how far Seneca was cognisant of
this conspiracy must remain uncertain, nor does
Tacitus express an opinion on the subject. That
the friend of Piso, the uncle of Lucan, would
have rejoiced at its success we cannot doubt,
just as Cicero rejoiced at the Ides of March.
But, like Cicero, he was probably not consulted

beforehand, and even if the evidence drawn by fear of torture from Scevinus was accurate, it only went to show that he was indirectly sounded on Piso's behalf and returned an ambiguous answer. We are told, indeed, by the untrustworthy historian Dion Cassius that Seneca was deeply concerned in the conspiracy, and that he declared that it was necessary to rescue the State from Nero and Nero from himself, but this seems to be merely an adapted quotation of a general maxim in the treatise *De Vita Beata.* However this may be, the discovery of the plot proved the ruin of Seneca, for it gave Nero the long-coveted opportunity of effecting the destruction of a mentor whom he hated ever the more the more he departed from his precepts and merited a disapproval which was not concealed.

The remainder of the story may be transcribed without paraphrase from Tacitus, since, if we except the brief and malignant narrative of Dion—an historian who ever gives proof of an envious dislike of great men and a desire to belittle them—he is the only extant authority for the last scene of Seneca's life.[1]

Then came the death of Annaeus Seneca, which gave great joy to Nero : not that he had any clear evidence of his guilt, but because he could now do by the sword what he had failed to do by poison. The sole witness against him was Natalis, and his evidence only came to this, that he had been sent to see Seneca when ill, and to complain of his refusing to see Piso : ' It would be better,' he had said, ' for such old friends to

---

[1] I have ventured to borrow Mr. G. G. Ramsay's excellent translation.

keep up their habits of intercourse.' To this Seneca had replied : ' Frequent meetings and conversations would do neither of them any good : but his own welfare depended on Piso's safety.'

Gavius Silvanus, Tribune of a Praetorian Cohort, was ordered to take the report of this incident to Seneca, and to ask him, ' Whether he admitted the correctness of the question of Natalis, and of his own answer to it ? ' Either by chance or purposely, it happened that Seneca was returning on that day from Campania, and had halted at a suburban villa four miles from Rome. Thither, towards evening, the tribune proceeded ; and having surrounded the house with soldiers, he delivered the emperor's message to Seneca when he was at table with his wife Pompeia Paulina and two friends.

Seneca's reply was : ' Natalis had been sent to complain on behalf of Piso that he was not permitted to visit him ; and he had tendered in excuse the state of his health and his love of quiet. As to his reason for regarding the welfare of a private individual as of more value than his own safety, he had had none. He was not a man addicted to flattery : and that no one knew better than Nero himself, who had more often found him too free than too servile in his utterances.' On receiving this report from the tribune in the presence of Poppaea and Tigellinus, who formed the emperor's inner council of cruelty, Nero asked, ' Was Seneca preparing to put an end to himself ? ' The tribune declared that he had observed no sign of alarm or dejection in Seneca's face or language. He was therefore ordered to go back and tell him he must die. Fabius Rusticus states that the tribune did not return by the same road by which he had come, but that he went out of his way to see Faenius, the prefect ; and having shown him Caesar's order, asked him, ' Should he obey it ? ' and that Faenius, with that fatal weakness which had come over them all, told him to execute his orders. For Silvanus himself was one of the conspirators, and he was now adding one more crime to those which he

M

had conspired to avenge. But he spared his own eyes and tongue, sending in one of the centurions to announce to Seneca that his last hour was come.

Seneca, undismayed, asked for his will ; but this the centurion refused. Then turning to his friends, he called them to witness that, ' Being forbidden to requite them for their services, he was leaving to them the sole, and yet the noblest, possession that remained to him— the pattern of his life. If they bore that in mind, they would win for themselves a name for virtue as the reward of their devoted friendship.' At one moment he would check their tears with conversation ; at another he would brace up their courage by high-strung language of rebuke, asking, ' Where was now their philosophy ? Where was that attitude towards the future which they had rehearsed for so many years ? To whom was Nero's cruelty unknown ? What was left for one who had murdered his mother and his brother but to slay his guardian and teacher also ? '

Having discoursed thus as if to the whole company, he embraced his wife, and abating somewhat of his tone of high courage, he implored her to moderate her grief, and not cling to it for ever : ' Let the contemplation of her husband's life of virtue afford her noble solace in her bereavement.'

She, however, announced her resolve to die with him ; and called on the operator to do his part. Seneca would not thwart her noble ambition ; and he loved her too dearly to expose her to insult after he was gone. ' I have pointed out to thee,' he said, ' how thou mayest soothe thy life ; but if thou prefer a noble death, I will not begrudge thee the example. Let us both share the fortitude of thus nobly dying : but thine shall be the nobler end.'

A single incision with the knife opened the arm of each, but as Seneca's aged body, reduced by spare living, would scarcely let the blood escape, he opened the veins of his knees and ankles also. Worn out at last by the pain, and fearing to break down his wife's courage by his suffering, or to lose his own self-command at the sight of hers, he begged her to move into another chamber. But even in his last moments his eloquence did not fail ; he called his secretaries to his side, and dictated to them many things which being published in his own words I deem it needless to reproduce.

Nero, however, had no personal dislike to Paulina ; and, not wishing to add to his character for cruelty, he ordered her death to be stayed. So, at the bidding of the soldiers, the slaves and freedmen tied up her arms and stopped the flow of blood ; perhaps she was unconscious. But with that alacrity to accept the worst version of a thing which marks the vulgar, some believed that so long as she thought Nero would be implacable she clutched at the glory of sharing her husband's death ; but that when the hope of a reprieve presented itself the attractions of life proved too strong for her. She lived on for a few years more, worthily cherishing her husband's memory ; but the pallor of her face and limbs showed how much vitality had gone out of her.

Meanwhile Seneca, in the agonies of a slow and lingering death, implored Statius Annaeus, his tried and trusted friend and physician, to produce a poison with which he had long provided himself, being the same as that used for public executions at Athens. The draught was brought and administered, but to no purpose ; the limbs were too cold, the body too numb, to let the poison act. At last, he was put into a warm bath ; and as he sprinkled the slaves about him he added : ' This libation is to Jupiter the Liberator ! ' He was then carried into the hot vapour bath, and perished of suffocation. His body was burnt without any funeral ceremony, in accordance with instructions about his end which he had inserted in his will in the heyday of his wealth and power.

CHAPTER XIII

THE PHILOSOPHY OF SENECA

THE practical and unsystematic character of
Seneca's philosophy makes it less easy to describe
than to understand. Its chief aim was the formation of character, and his pupils were taught to
possess their souls in peace by the acceptance,
so far as they were applicable to actual life, of
Stoic principles. Philosophy, he says, is not a
popular profession devised for ostentation or the
display of ingenuity ; it lies not in words, but in
realities. Nor do we pursue it in order to spend
our days agreeably or to banish weariness from
our leisure ; it cultivates and forms the mind,
orders life, guides our actions by showing us
what to do and what not to do, sits at the helm
and directs our course through the changes and
chances of the world. What is the one true
possession of man ? Himself, answers Seneca.
What is Liberty ?—to be the slave of no want,
of no chance, to meet Fortune on equal terms ;
but if a man desire or fear external things he is
so far the slave of him who has them to give or
to withhold.

Among the external things to be regarded objectively as neither good nor evil in themselves, save through the opinion we form of them, must be reckoned in Seneca's philosophy our own bodies, in which as in boats we travel so strangely from port to port. In these bodies is sown the divine seed which develops or decays, according to the soil in which it is planted and the cultivation it receives. If the seed prospers and a reasonable soul is engendered this is the real man-spirit still cleaving, like a sun-ray, to its divine origin, and his body but the case in which the jewel lies, indispensable certainly to his appearance in the physical world, as the instrument is indispensable to the heard melody, but no more the source from which he springs than the violin on which it is played is that of a sonata of Beethoven, or the ground on which the sun's rays shine is that of light.[1] This complete separation in thought of our spiritual selves from the few pounds of matter in which we are clothed, and through which we act and suffer, lies at the root of the Stoic conception of happiness and wisdom, which indeed in their opinion are the same. We are only as miserable as we think ourselves. We are free, because all our actions are in our own power, and if we are ready to sacrifice our external possessions, including among them our bodies, rather than lose this freedom, it cannot be taken from us. Other men

---

[1] 'Animus : sed hic rectus, bonus, magnus. Quid aliud voces hunc, quam Deum in humano corpore hospitantem ? Hic animus tam in equitem Romanum, quam in libertinum, quam in servum potest cadere. Quid est eques Romanus, aut libertinus, aut servus ? Nomina ex ambitione, aut ex injuria nata' (*Ep.* 31).

may have power over our bodies—indeed every man has that if he chooses to exert it without regard to consequences—they can have none over ourselves. '*Vindica te tibi*'—claim to be lord of yourself, make good your claim to be free for your own sake, subject not your will to another's, wrote Seneca in the first of his letters to Lucilius, and the remaining series are largely a commentary on that text.

Philosophy, as Seneca understood it, is the study of the works of God and of the nature of man ; of natural science and of the moral law. He would have understood and assented to the saying of the modern sage who declared that the two great subjects of his admiration and reverence were the starry heaven outside him and the moral law within. Man's nature he held to be twofold—an inherited instinctive or physical nature which he shares with the animals, and a rational nature which is divine. The last is the proper or distinguishing character of man, and only so far as it gains the mastery can he truly be said as man to live. The end of philosophy is to secure this predominance, and so far as it succeeds in so doing man is placed beyond the power of Fortune and his felicity is assured. His good and evil reside in the choice which it is always in his power to make. External things— his own body included—are in themselves neither good nor evil, but they are the material out of which man makes the one or the other. ' They reach not unto the soul,' as Marcus Aurelius says, ' but stand without still and quiet, and it is from the opinion only which is within that all the tumult and all the trouble doth proceed.' It is excellent, wrote Seneca, to combine the freedom from concern of a God with the physical frailty of man.[1] All nature is one. We are all members of a single great body.[2]   In the physical world this is clear to the view, for the actual material of which it is composed is used successively for all things—for minerals, for plants, and for animals.   But it is also true of the spiritual world to which man alone of living things has been granted admission.   Hence it follows that we are called by our spiritual nature to recognise our universal kinship and to love one another, hence come our notions of equity and justice, and a belief which consciously or unconsciously we must hold that it is better for a man to be wronged than to wrong.

Thus Seneca was a dualist.   For him, as has been said, there is the world of matter of which our bodies are a part, and there is the world of spirit which is divine.   Bodies are the instruments of our free action when we possess ourselves, but when we obey their behests we lose our freedom and become the slaves of those who can threaten us with or save us from the perils to which the body is exposed—poverty, sickness, or external violence.   Of these we dread the last most because of its tumultuous onset, whereas the others creep silently upon us accompanied by nothing formid-

[1] *Ep.* 53 : 'Ecce res magna, habere imbecillitatem hominis, securitatem Dei.'

[2] *Ep.* 95 : 'Omne hoc quod vides, quo divina et humana conclusa sunt, unum est : membra sumus corporis magni.'

able to our eyes or ears. Yet there is no difference in respect of the sole physical realities—pain and death. It was a Stoic maxim that the good of man lies in a certain regulation of his choice with regard to the appearances of things ; and it is only in the spiritual world that this faculty of choice can be said to exist. So far as the body controls the human will in its own interests— answering with corresponding reactions the stroke of its perceptions and sensations—that will is determined and becomes the servant of what it should command. To obey the orders of the body is to serve another's will and to surrender that true liberty which to the Stoic was life itself. Again and again Seneca recurs to this thesis :

My dearest Lucilius [he writes], do, I beseech you, the one thing that can make you happy. Scatter and tread under foot all those extrinsic splendours which hang on the promises of others ; look to the true good, and rejoice in what is your own. And what is that ? Yourself, and the best part of yourself. This little body, even though nothing can be done without it, is rather a necessary than a great matter.[1]

My body [he says in another letter] I regard but as a chain by which my liberty is fettered. I offer it therefore to Fortune as an object for her attacks ; nor through this shield do I allow myself to be pierced. In this is all my vulnerable part ; this frail and exposed house does my soul inhabit inviolate. This flesh shall never constrain me to fear or unworthy simulation. Let me never lie for the sake of this poor carcase.[2]

[1] *Ep.* 23.
[2] *Ep.* 65 : ' Nunquam me caro ista compellet ad metum ; nunquam ad indignam bono simulationem ; *nunquam in honorem hujus corpusculi mentiar.*'

In Seneca's view a man cannot be said to live a man's life who does not serve his own will. He becomes an automaton acted on by the material world outside him, on which he himself in his turn reacts. True he cannot live for himself unless he live for others,[1] for we are all children of the same Father, all members of one great body ; but it is of his own free will that he must live for others, and not through submission of his will to theirs. All action is really voluntary. No man need be a slave who is ready to take the consequences to his body—pain or death at the most—of a refusal to serve. The doctrine of the divine immanence was held by Seneca as firmly as was possible to an understanding so sceptical and an imagination so mobile, and it lies at the root of his theory of life.

There is no need to raise our hands to heaven [he tells Lucilius] or to prevail upon the keeper of the temple to admit us to the presence of the image, as if by such means our prayers were more likely to be heard. God is near you, He is with you, He is within you. I tell you, Lucilius, the Holy Spirit abides within us,[2] watching over and guarding our good or evil destiny : as we treat Him, so He treats us. No good man is without God. Can any unassisted by Him rise above Fortune ? Lofty and sublime are His counsels. In every good man God dwells, though what God is uncertain. . . . If you see a man unmoved by danger, unaffected by desires, happy in adversity, calm in the midst of tempests, looking at men from a higher station, at the gods from a level,

----

[1] ' Qui sibi amicus est, scito hunc amicum omnibus esse ' (*Ep.* 6). ' Alteri vivas oportet, si tibi vis vivere ' (*Ep.* 48).

[2] ' Sacer intra nos spiritus sedet, malorum bonorumque nostrorum observator et custos.'

will you feel no veneration for him ? Will you not say, Here is something so great and so sublime that it is incredible he should resemble the little body in which he dwells ? . . . Just as the rays of the sun reach indeed the earth yet are still in the place whence they are transmitted : so a great and sacred soul sent down to the earth, that we might have closer knowledge of divine things, holds intercourse indeed with us but cleaves to its own origin.[1]

At the same time Seneca was no believer in extreme asceticism—a practice which he regarded as a confusion of means with end. The body is not to be indulged, lest like an overfed horse it should get out of hand ; but since it is our instrument of action, our only means of communication with the outside world, since through it we enter into relations with the external things that form the materials on which, and the medium through which, our choice can be exercised, we are to regard it as a useful servant, and to clothe, clean, protect, and maintain it in a manner suitable to its nature and with a view to its highest efficiency. It is a tool which we are to keep in good condition, a house to be kept in repair ; but we must ever be careful not to confound the tool with the workman, the house with its inhabitant.

Seneca held, as we have seen, that man's characteristic excellence and peculiar attribute is his reason, which is nothing but a part of the divine nature sunk in a human body.[2] Therefore to follow reason is to act according to his nature ; just as for other animals to follow the lead of their bodies is to act after their kind. It is

---

[1] *Ep.* 41.   [2] *Ep.* 64.

opposed to his physical, inherited, or irrational
self in respect of which he belongs to the world
of matter.   Though this latter part of him has the
greater dynamic power, and has ever been the
source of the greater number of human actions,
yet inasmuch as body and the necessary actions
that proceed from bodily affections or passions—
whether hunger, fear, or lust—are not peculiar
to human beings but are common to them and
all other animals, we do not speak of them as
natural to man.   Such words as 'humanity' and
'kindness,' recurring as they do in many languages,
point to this distinction.   It was ever in the
mind of the Roman Stoics, and is the foundation
upon which many of their seeming paradoxes rest.

In one of the very few allusions to Seneca to be
found in the writings of his actual contemporaries,
we are told by the elder Pliny that no man was
less beguiled by the appearances of things—
'minime mirator inanium'—and this indeed is
just what we might infer from his works.   In spite
of the rhetoric by which they are sometimes
adorned, and sometimes disfigured, we hear and
recognise a familiar human voice in reading his
letters.   The sense of remoteness which we feel
towards writers of past generations is proportioned
to the greater or less degree in which their nature
was subdued to the transient humours of the
time in which they worked.   Shakespeare could
perceive and describe these humours—the strings
by which human puppets are moved—as clearly
as Ben Jonson, but because he could also perceive
and describe the universal humanity that lies

at the back of them, because he recognises the something in every man that either controls or checks or yields to them, his characters seem to us modern and natural, and Jonson's, because he cannot do this, mechanical and obsolete. Seneca, with his constant desire to see with his own eyes things as they are and not as they are reputed to be —to remove the mask from things as well as from persons—has the same power.[1] We never have to plead the opinions of his time as an apology for any opinion he holds. We may agree with him or disagree, but it is a living voice we hear—never a mere echo. For Reason being universal and absolute, independent of time and place, and of the humours of mankind, the voice of Reason, no matter from what distance of space or time, reaches us as a living voice. We feel our kindred with the speaker however great an interval may separate us from his physical presence. We recognise and greet in him our common nature, for this is the true nature of man, the λόγος—the ' spirit ' of the New Testament as opposed to the ' flesh,' the seed, the new birth, the divine spark, the real humanity.

Seneca defines wisdom as constancy of will— '*semper idem velle atque idem nolle.*' There is no danger, he adds, lest this constancy should have a wrong object, since it is impossible that anything but what is right should at all times please us. There must be but one same efficient motive to

---

[1] *Ep.* 24 : ' Illud ante omnia memento, demere rebus tumultum, ac videre quid in quaque re sit : scies nihil esse in istis terribile nisi ipsum timorem.—Non hominibus tantum, sed et rebus persona demenda est, et reddenda facies sua.'

all our actions, and we shall never regret them whatever their results. Actions, like things, are in themselves neither good nor bad—it is the manner and the circumstances that qualify them. The very same action is base or honourable, according to the mental disposition of the actor. A man attends assiduously the sick bed of his friend, and we approve. But if he does this with a view to an inheritance, we regard him as a vulture awaiting his prey. The action is the same in both cases, but in the first we recognise what we significantly call the man's humanity, that is, goodness, truth, and beauty, those fruits of the universal human spirit, of which man could not have formed the idea were they not the very material of his reasonable soul ; and our consciousness of the self-regarding source of the same action in the other case fills us with a certain disgust. As with things so with actions, we must weigh them without regard to their reputation, and consider not what they are called but what they are.

Notwithstanding his rhetoric and antitheses, it is this recall to reality which is the dominant note in Seneca's writings. An excellent critic, who was by no means an undiscriminating admirer of his subject, has written : ' The less a man cares for the practical, the real, the less he will value Seneca. The more a man envelops himself in words and ideas without exact meaning, the less will he comprehend a writer who does not merely deal in words, but has ideas with something to correspond to them.'[1] Seneca

[1] G. Long.

had the contempt of a man of the world for pedantry, though the impatience with pure speculation that he felt as an ethical instructor was tempered in some degree by his own insatiable curiosity. 'We sometimes find,' he wrote in one of his letters, 'that the pursuit of liberal arts makes men tedious, wordy, unreasonable, self-satisfied, and ignorant of what they should know, just because they have learnt what is needless.'[1] Philosophy, in his view, is the science of reality, 'the knowledge of which the gods have given to none,' he tells us, 'but the power of attainment to all. Had they indeed made this a common possession, had we been born wise, wisdom would have lost her chief excellence and have been subject to Fortune, whereas it is her most precious and noble quality that she falls of herself to no man's lot, that each man owes her to himself, and seeks her from no other.'[2] This acquisition of 'self-control in accordance with fixed principles that are self-prescribed' forms what is called character, which, as Kant remarks, implies a subject conscious of something which he has himself acquired. The man who possesses it is free, for he is the slave of nothing—of no want, of no chance; he meets Fortune on equal terms and can do what he pleases, for nothing pleases him that he ought not to do. The philosopher sees things as they are presented to him by nature, not as they are represented to him by his imagination worked on by the suggestion of others. 'Above all things, remember,' writes

[1] *Ep.* 88.   [2] *Ep.* 90.

Seneca, ' to strip things of their glamour and to contemplate each as it is in itself : you will find that they contain nothing formidable but your own fear.'[1] ' *Non effectus sed efficientia timor spectat*,' he says elsewhere ; it is the pomp and circumstance of pain and death (the only positive physical evils), not pain and death themselves, which we fear, that is, from which we suffer in anticipation. We think death the greatest of evils, when the only evil connected with it is one which vanishes on its appearance, namely, the terror it inspires. We are indignant and complain, and do not perceive that the only reality of ill is to be found in our indignation and complaints.

To have a right judgment in all things it is sufficient to have our own judgment (or perception of the differences between things) unbiased by that of others ; then we acquire the inestimable boon of becoming lords of ourselves. When a man serves his own will and not other persons or things he will do right, because he then acts on general principles ; and general thoughts are just. No man is a rogue for the pleasure of being a rogue, but to gain some end which seems to him a good one, but which to the philosopher would not seem worth a struggle were it even attainable innocently. The slave of his passions may fancy that in serving them he is serving his own will ; but it is not so, for he has lost his self-control and must obey those who are able to gratify or not to gratify those passions. He is, as Hamlet

[1] *Ep.* 24.

says, ' a pipe for Fortune's finger to sound what stop she please.' One gift, says Seneca, we have from Nature, and that is, that the light of virtue is visible to all ; even those who do not follow perceive it ; but if we are not distracted by the false opinions of things suggested to us from outside or by our own bodily selves, to perceive and to follow the light will be all one.[1]

Stoicism in the centuries before Christ was like a motor started but off the clutch. There is a great deal of potential energy, but being merely potential it results in nothing but noise. Seneca supplied the clutch to Stoicism by applying it to the practical conduct of life, and he was followed in this work by Epictetus and Marcus Aurelius. Thus a statesman, a slave, and an emperor, differing as widely in temperament as they did in position, reached, nevertheless, the same conclusions as to the nature of man and the secret of his felicity. What the Greeks preach, the Romans practise, says Quintilian—a greater matter.[2] As was natural to one who had lived in the centre of things and seen much of men and affairs, Seneca felt little but disdain for the logical and metaphysical puzzles which occupied so much of the time and thought of the earlier Greek philosophers and schoolmen, and which seem to have had a great attraction for his Epicurean friend, Lucilius. He reproaches philosophers with teaching how to dispute rather than how to live, and their pupils with attending

---

[1] *De Beneficiis*, 7.17.
[2] ' Quantum enim Graeci praeceptis valent, tantum Romani (quod est majus) exemplis ' (Quintilian, xii. 2).

lectures in order to sharpen their wits rather than improve their characters.   The most mischievous of mortals he declares to be those who bring their philosophy to market and by not practising what they preach seem a living proof of the futility of their doctrines.   He argues with force against those who maintained the sufficiency of general principles and the needlessness of precepts for their application to the conduct of life.   Virtue, he says, consists partly in theory and partly in practice ; you ought both to learn and to make good what you have learnt by your actions.   If this is so, the precepts of wisdom are of service as well as her decrees ; they issue, as it were, edicts by which our affections are bound and constrained.

The earlier philosophers were so occupied with the form of the human understanding that they neglected its material content.   The driving power was supplied but continued unlinked to the engine to be driven.   Seneca, too, considered the external world but as the material of wise men— the ball, not prized for its own sake, on which the player is to exercise his skill—but to show the bearing of this discovery on the actual circumstances of life and action seemed to him the main business of philosophy.

Not out of ivory only [he tells us] was Phidias skilled in making statues, he made them of bronze; if you brought marble or any cheaper material to him he would turn it to the best use of which it was capable. So, if riches fall to him, the wise man will display his wisdom amidst riches, if not, then in poverty; if he can, in his native country, if not, then in exile; if he can, as a general, if not, then as a soldier ; if he can, in health, if not, then in sickness. Whatever fortune befall him, he will carve out of it something memorable.[1]

The lives of most men are passed in a perpetual struggle to improve the external circumstances of their lives ; either their reputations—that is, the opinions held of them by other people—or their fortunes—that is, their power of directing the labour of other people to the satisfaction of their own desires and caprices. Thus for the sake of an imagined life they lose their real life. Could we recognise that the attainment of these objects is not in our own power, and that even if by the aid of Fortune they are attained they bring no real happiness with them, but only through their transitory nature disillusionment, we should accept the chances and circumstances of our lives without perturbation or care, use them as it befits us to use them with the same tendency whatever they are, and be at peace.

Seneca was a man of quick sympathies, impressionable, witty, and amiable, humane, fastidious, and full of good sense, interested perhaps in man rather than in men, yet devoted to his friends, and combining a desire to please and success in pleasing, with a love of nature and solitary meditation. He was a citizen of the world,[2] who could take a detached view of men and things, and his generous conviction that distinctions of rank and status had their origin in opinion, itself the child of fortune, and in the names in

[1] *Ep.* 85.
[2] ' Non sum uni angulo natus : patria mea totus hic est mundus.'

which that opinion was registered rather than in
any real superiority or inferiority, often led him
to anticipate the ideas of a very distant future.
Quintilian describes him as no great philosopher
(' *in philosophia parum diligens* '), but praises him
as a moral instructor of distinction whose works
are to be studied—by those able to sift the good
from the bad—for the sake of the striking thoughts
with which they abound. He allows him a ready
wit, flowing perhaps too easily from a perennial
source, industry, and a wide knowledge of natural
history, though he remarks that he was sometimes misled by those whom he had commissioned
to make investigations ; but with all this he charges
him with an absolute lack of judgment and with
being the chief corrupter of eloquence and intro-
ducer of new methods in composition which utterly
unfitted him to guide the taste of the youth
of his generation, in whose hands for a time
his books alone were to be found. He denounces
him, indeed, as a sort of literary anarchist, whose
influence on the manner of his age was disastrous,
and having once again admitted that there was
much in his works to approve, much even to admire, by those who could distinguish (and for those
whose taste was sufficiently formed this, he says,
would be good practice), he sums up his criticism
with the remark that it was a pity one capable
of doing what he pleased should not more often
have been pleased with better things.[1] Quintilian,

---

[1] ' Digna enim fuit illa natura, quae meliora vellet, quae quod
voluit effecit.' One is reminded of Jonson's reply to Shakespeare's
fellow-players, who boasted that he had never blotted a line,
' Would he had blotted a thousand.'

on conventional lines, was one of the best critics
that have ever passed judgment on the works
of others—the Sainte-Beuve of his age. But
Seneca was in literature a revolutionary, with a
dislike of convention, scant respect for tradition,
and impatience of authority[1]; and Quintilian,
the classicist, was of opinion that he owed his
popularity not to his good qualities—the '*multae
et magnae virtutes*' which he freely recognised—
but to his dangerously attractive faults—his
rhetoric and his detached sentences, good, bad,
and indifferent, not woven according to the rules
of art into the texture of a complete work, but
scattered in careless profusion as they occurred
to him and lying where they fell. For Roman
conservatives such as Quintilian, Roman citizenship
was a primary consideration, and for a Roman
citizen moral obligations were in large measure
confined to their relations with their fellow-
citizens. For Seneca, on the other hand, and his
school, man was sacred to man as man [2]—the idea of
citizenship with its rights and duties was swallowed
up and lost in that of humanity, all men were
brothers and sprang from the same origin.[3] The
most useful life a man could lead was spent in
helping, teaching, and consoling his fellow-men
—be they Romans or barbarians, free or slave.
The maxims in which Seneca enshrined these
notions seemed to Quintilian rhetorical commonplace calculated to please children and of a sub-

---

[1] *Ep.* 33: 'Non sumus sub rege, sibi quisque se vindicet.'

[2] *Ep.* 95: 'Homo res sacra homini.'

[3] Cp. his contemporary, Pliny, ii. 7: 'Deus est mortali juvare mortalem'; and St. Paul *passim*.

versive tendency. Such ideas, he may have thought, might be suited to the schools of declamation; but introduced into serious treatises and found in conjunction with much that was really just and wise, they could not be too strongly condemned.

Was Seneca the author of the tragedies which bear his name ? That they were written by him or by one of his family we know from the quotation by Quintilian of an extant line of the *Medea*,[1] while other mentions are made of the tragedies of 'Seneca' by the grammarians of the second century —Terentianus Maurus, and Valerius Probus. It is evident, however, that one of the plays, the *Octavia*, cannot have been written by Lucius Seneca, who appears in it as a principal character, since it contains in the guise of a prophecy a fairly accurate description of the death of Nero.[2]

Conceding this, most modern writers have nevertheless attributed the remaining eight tragedies to the philosopher. Yet apart from the fact that there seems no sufficient reason for separating the *Octavia* from the rest of the collection, the case against his authorship seems to me so strong as to be almost conclusive. Quintilian, in his account of Roman writers of tragedy from Accius and Pacuvius down to Pomponius Secundus, whom he had known personally, makes no mention of Seneca. This, if at the time he was writing Seneca

---

[1] ' Interrogamus, aut invidiae gratia : ut Medea apud Senecam —"quas peti terras jubes ? "' (Quint. ix. 2. 8).

[2] ' Veniet dies tempusque, quo reddat suis
Animam nocentem sceleribus, jugulum hostibus,
Desertus, et destructus, et cunctis egens.'
Oct. 629–631.

the tragedian were actually alive, is comprehensible, for Quintilian avoids all criticism of his living contemporaries, and only alludes without naming him to Tacitus himself. But if Lucius Seneca were the author of the plays, how could he have passed him over in silence ? Moreover, he tells us that Lucius Seneca practised almost every form of literature, leaving behind him orations, poems, epistles, and dialogues. Why no mention of the tragedies ? But the strongest external reason for disbelieving in the identity of Seneca the tragedian with Seneca the philosopher is to be found in the poem of Sidonius Apollinaris, written in the fifth century, in which he distinguishes between the two.[1] It is difficult to believe that Sidonius, to whom letters were the chief interest in life, and who lived in an age before the final break up of the Empire had cast a doubt on so many origins, could have been mistaken on such a point. He writes, too, as he naturally would if no question on the subject had been raised, as if the matter were one of common knowledge.

As to the internal evidence, the defects of Seneca are visible in the plays, tempered by few

[1] ' Non quod Corduba praepotens alumnis
Facundum ciet, hic putes legendum :
Quorum unus colit hispidum Platona,
Incassumque suum monet Neronem :
Orchestram quatit alter Euripidis,
Pictum faecibus Aeschylum secutus
Aut plaustris solitum sonare Thespin :
Qui post pulpita trita sub cothurno
Ducebant olidae matrem capellae.'
Carm. ix.
Cp. *Carm.* xxiii. : ' Quid celsos Senecas loquar.'

of his better qualities.   Quintilian says of the later writers of that school, that all they can do is to imitate and exaggerate the faults and mannerisms of their master, since his real excellence is beyond their capacity.   By resembling they, so to speak, slander him.[1]   I do not dwell upon the absence of all allusion to the tragedies in his letters, though he quotes Euripides and Publius, for Seneca was completely free from that literary vanity which was so conspicuous in Cicero, and in no one of his letters does he mention any other of his works.   Indeed, with the exception of a single passage in his twenty-first letter, in which with a certain solemnity he promises Lucilius that as Idomeneus lives for ever in the letters of Epicurus, Atticus in those of Cicero, so it was also in his power to confer immortality on his own correspondent, we hear nothing of his great position and reputation from himself.

The denunciations of tyrants and tyranny with which the plays abound, and the direct references, as they appear to be, to Seneca's own relations with Nero which they contain, have appeared to M. Boissier conclusive evidence of his authorship. But they also make it in a high degree unlikely that the plays were published during Nero's lifetime, and would rather indicate their publication under Vespasian by another member of Seneca's family. ' He who distributes crowns at his will,' we read in the *Thyestes*, ' before whom trembling nations bend the knee, who by a sign of his hand disarms

[1] One wonders whether he may not have had Seneca the tragedian among others in his mind when so writing.

Medes, Indians, and tribes dreaded of the Parthians, is himself uneasy on his throne ; he shudders at the thought of the caprices of fortune and of the unforeseen strokes by which empires are overthrown.'[1] Again, in the same play, 'Believe me, we are deceived by the glozing surface of prosperity, and we are wrong indeed to regret its loss. While I was powerful, I never ceased to tremble ; but now I can cause fear or jealousy to none, I am happy. Crime does not seek out the poor man in his hut. He dines at a modest table, whereas we run the risk of poison when we drink from golden goblets. I speak from experience.'[2] It is evident that the writer of these passages had Nero and Seneca in his mind ; Seneca had indeed experienced the danger he describes,[3] but that he would have published or even committed to writing such sentiments in the tyrant's lifetime is hard to believe. Who, then, can be the author of the plays ? Seneca's brothers did not long survive him. His nephew Lucan was condemned ; and as the blood spurted from his opened veins with his dying voice he declaimed a passage from the *Pharsalia* descriptive of his situation. His father, Mela, claimed his estate ; but the claim was contested by Lucan's intimate friend, Fabius Romanus, who professed to find among the papers left him letters involving Mela in the conspiracy. This was enough for Nero, who coveted Mela's great wealth, and a message was sent him, with the usual result. He at once anticipated a condemnation by opening his veins, leaving behind him a will

[1] *Thyestes*, 600. [2] *Ibid.*, 446. [3] Tac., *Ann.* xv. 45.

in which he bequeathed a great sum of money to Tigellinus, in the hope that by interesting the prefect in the validity of the document his remaining legacies might be secured to his family. That he was successful in this is probable, because a generation later we find Lucan's widow, Polla, living wealthy and honoured under Domitian, and receiving the seldom disinterested attentions of the Flavian poets. Gallio, after Seneca's death, was violently attacked in the Senate ; but saved for the moment by friends, who reproached his antagonist with taking advantage of the public misfortunes for the gratification of private hatred and opposing the humane impulses of their merciful prince. We hear no more of him from Tacitus ; but Dion relates that he perished shortly afterwards by his own hand. The only other Seneca of whom any mention has survived is Marcus, the son of the philosopher, of whom he wrote so tenderly from his Corsican exile. Can he have been the dramatist ? Nothing obliges us to believe it ; but it is possible, and has been believed.

Seneca's reputation has passed through many vicissitudes. He has been long neglected, and his character when discussed has been harshly appreciated. Yet good wine cannot come from a tainted vessel ; and if we judge his work by the use that has been made of it by famous poets and moralists, we must call it a noble heritage. Shakespeare and Milton have transmuted many of his thoughts into glorious poetry—Milton taking directly from him, Shakespeare in all

probability by way of Florio's Montaigne. From
the first he has excited admiration and hostility
in almost equal measure. He is perhaps the
only pagan whom the early Christian writers—
Tertullian, Augustine, Lactantius, and Jerome—
regarded with all but unmixed approval. On
the other hand, the pedantic Roman archaists of
the Antonine period—Aulus Gellius and Fronto—
detested him as the corrupter of taste and a
dangerous innovator. It must always be remembered that his was no abstract philosophy of the
study. It was addressed by a former man of
action to men living under a reign of terror,
whose lives were in daily peril; and its object was
to free them from anxiety and brace their minds
to meet their fate with indifference and dignity.
Consequently it is in dangerous times that he
has found the greatest favour.

CAIUS MAECENAS

CAIUS MAECENAS

THE battle of Actium had been fought and won.
For the third time in Roman history the gates of
the Temple of Janus were closed as a sign that
war had ceased. After a century of civil war and
confusion the Romans accepted, some of them
with joy, others with a half-ashamed relief, others
again with melancholy resignation, the repose
and security offered to them by the new government. The historian Livy, whom the emperor
was accustomed playfully to tax with his Pom-
peian sympathies, turned, as he tells us, to the
composition of Roman history and the contemplation of the ancient glories of the State in order
to distract his mind from what seemed to him
the incurable degeneracy of the times. Horace,
who had served as an officer under Brutus at
Philippi, took refuge in Epicurean philosophy
and the cultivation of friendship, while he advised
his friends to rid themselves of hopes and fears,
to make the best of the passing hour, and not to
trouble about the future. We must all die : so
what, after all, does anything matter ? is the
constant burden of his song. Reconciliation and

oblivion were the order of the day. To the son of that Cicero, the thunder of whose eloquence in defence of the old constitution had cost him his life, fell the duty as consul of announcing to the people the news of the battle of Actium and of presiding over the games and pageants given in honour of the victory. The untamable soul of Cato was applauded with impunity by the Court poets. Men, like Messala, who had distinguished themselves on the republican side in the civil war were admitted to the intimacy of the emperor; and the letter of the old constitution was preserved inviolate at a time when its spirit was fundamentally subverted.

Augustus seems really to have been by temperament a conservative. He cared little for the pomp and circumstance of power, and was under no temptation to imitate those excesses of unconstitutional language and demeanour, the fatal candour of which had proved more disastrous to his uncle Julius Caesar than the most violent of his actions. He knew that wounded vanity is a more potent factor in the making of patriots than loss of liberty. Moreover, he was attached to the Roman traditions and religion; he was a lover of order, system, and decorum; he had the historical sense; he had an admirable taste in literature; he was an indulgent friend; and he loved the freedom from restraint in social intercourse secured with such difficulty by princes.

When Augustus returned from his final victory at Actium, he contemplated a genuine

restoration of the republic ; and to this course
he was urged by his most powerful lieutenant,
Marcus Agrippa. But he was dissuaded from
adopting it by his other chief adviser, the Tuscan
knight, Caius Maecenas, who, left in charge of
the city while the emperor was still absent, had
recently increased his influence by his skilful sup-
pression in its inception of a conspiracy against
his master's life, formed by Lepidus, the son of
the triumvir.[1]

The character of this celebrated man is in
itself an interesting study ; and, typically differing as it does from that of all the public men
in earlier Roman history, it enables us to appreciate
more clearly the nature of the change that came
over Roman life after the accession of Augustus
to sole power, and to weigh with more intelligence the advantages and disadvantages of that
change.

Maecenas, in the first place, was a great realist. He professed and probably felt nothing but
disdain for all good and evil derived not from
things themselves, but from the opinions men
form of them. Thus, though proud of his old
Etruscan lineage, he would never consent to enter
the Senate or to hold the official honours—now
become in the main titular—of praetor or consul.
He died as he was born in the equestrian order.
It is indeed possible that his moderation in this
matter was in part a compliment to the emperor, who, himself descended from an equestrian
family in which his father had been the first

<hr />

[1] Vell. Paterculus, ii. 88 ; Appian, iv. 49.

senator, was not at all ashamed to avow the fact
in his published memoirs[1]; and this theory
receives some support from the circumstance
that the successor of Maecenas in the confidence
of Augustus, Crispus Sallustius, followed his example in this respect, as he did in his luxurious
way of living—'*diversus a veterum instituto*'[2]—
and in his Melbournesque pose of indolence and
indifference. None the less were his contemporaries astonished by the modesty of Maecenas,
there being no prior instance in Roman history of
a public man who enjoyed all the reality without
any of the titular distinctions of power. Whatever its real origin, this much-commended abstention from the honours of the State can have
caused the statesman little effort. His pene-
trating vision pierced through the appearances of
things to their essence, and so all those dignities
which owed their importance to the vain opinions
of mortal men were to him as nothing. '*Nil
admirari prope res est una.*' Perhaps it was of
Maecenas that Horace was thinking when he
wrote that celebrated line.

His, again, was the tolerant temperament often
found to spring ˙from complete scepticism. Of
the substantial well-being of his fellow-men he
was sincerely desirous. But he did not think
this likely to be promoted by the restoration of
their ancient liberties. His good-nature, like
that of Sir Robert Walpole, was the child
of his low opinion of human nature—of his

---

[1] Suet., *Oct.* 2.   [2] Tac., *Ann.* iii. 30.

pessimism. He expected little from the virtues of others, and therefore felt no anger when their actions did not exceed his expectations. With idealism he had no sympathy. He cared for nothing but the actual and the tangible. The only way in which he showed his power, we are told by a hostile critic, was by doing as he pleased —by his contempt for appearances. Romans of the old school were shocked to see him lounging about the streets of Rome at a time when, in the absence of Augustus, his power in that city was absolute, with his robe hanging loosely about him and a hood pulled over his head leaving his ears exposed ; like a fugitive slave in a comedy, so they said.[1] For the fate of his body after death he felt a very characteristic indifference. ' *Nec tumulum curo : sepelit Natura relictos,*'[2] he wrote in one of the few lines of his poetry that have been preserved to us. What to him was a grave or a monument ? Life was the great reality ; death the negation of life. And accordingly he clung to life with a passionate and pathetic insistence which to the Stoic Seneca appeared *contemptissimus*, but from another point of view may even be regarded as heroic. ' Torture my body,' he cries in the well-known lines to Fortune, ' rack me with gout ; break and distort my limbs ; nail me to a cross ; grant me but Life, and it is well.' Seneca has generally been echoed, and these verses have been often quoted to show the innate effeminacy of Maecenas ; but how do they differ, save by inferior expression,

---

[1] Seneca, *Ep*. 114.   [2] Id., *Ep*. 92.

from the great lines which Milton puts into the
mouth of Belial ?

Who would lose,
Though full of pain, this intellectual being,
Those thoughts that wander through eternity,
To perish rather, swallowed up and lost
In the wide womb of uncreated night
Devoid of sense and motion ?

However, that Maecenas was really self-
indulgent and over-luxurious in his manner of
life is, of course, undeniable. All the Roman
authorities are agreed upon this point. Epicureanism was the fashionable philosophy of the
time, and there can be little doubt that of this
fashion the indolent statesman was a principal
leader. He disliked forms and despised conventions. The small Roman banquets, with their
wines and their sweet ointments, their music and
their roses, were clearly delightful to him. He
forgave the numerous infidelities of his beautiful
wife Terentia ; and although he often divorced
her he as often took her back, thinking perhaps
that to act otherwise would be to fling away the
substance of his pleasure for a shadow. But,
realist though he was, the fact that the emperor,
to whom he was sincerely attached, was among
her lovers appears to have troubled his declining
years. He forgave Augustus, nevertheless, and
bequeathed to him the greater part of his possessions. Velleius Paterculus tells us that though
provident and energetic enough when something
definite had to be done, as soon as the business
in hand ceased to be urgent he relapsed into an

indolence and softness more than feminine.[1] He
delighted in the games of the Campus Martius.
His friends he chose from inclination and without
respect of persons from among the poets and wits
of his time; his acquaintance with a view to
amusement. Horace describes a dinner-party at
the house of the rich *parvenu* Nasidienus at
which Maecenas was present attended by two
boon companions (*umbrae*). For the diversion
of the great man the pomposity and vanity of
the host were ruthlessly exploited by his two
followers under the forms of politeness; the
noise increased as the wine circulated; and the
feast came to an end amid riotous buffoonery.[2]
We see him, through the eyes of Propertius,
driving through Rome in a cunningly-wrought two-
wheeled chariot of a kind lately imported from
Britain[3]; while at other times he would forget
the cares of State and dine merrily with Horace
'*sine aulaeis et ostro*' at the Sabine farm which
the poet owed to his munificence.

The Palace of Art, the construction of which
as an habitation for his soul was the object of
Maecenas's later life, proved, as we shall see, but
a crumbling and unstable edifice. But in the
meantime it demanded a splendid material en-
vironment, and this he provided by his house and
gardens on the Esquiline. Here he transformed
the old Roman plebeian cemetery into a park,
famous through many succeeding generations;
and here he built a lofty tower, from the summit
of which he would spend hours in contemplating

[1] ii. 88.   [2] Hor., *Sat.* ii. 8.   [3] Prop. ii. 1.

the beautiful prospect of the Campagna with the slopes of Tibur in the distance and nearer at hand the fume and fret and riches of the Eternal City.[1] Maecenas was a valetudinarian, with a horror of death. He was a victim to acute insomnia. The elder Pliny assures us that for the last three years of his life he never enjoyed a moment's sleep[2]; and, quite incredible as this statement may be, even its approximate accuracy is quite enough to account for the ceaseless complaints with which, as we know from Horace, he was accustomed to overburden his friends. Ingenuity was exhausted to devise a remedy for this terrible affliction. The sound of falling waters, the choicest wines, the music of symphonies gently rising and falling in the distance— '*symphoniarum cantum ex longinquo lene resonantium*'—all were vain.[3] The tower itself— standing amid its vast gardens and orchards— was a centre of quiet. There Augustus took refuge when attacked by illness; thither came the unsocial and unhappy Tiberius to rest his eyes from the hated sight of his fellow-men; there Nero sang in costume the story of burning Troy as he watched with aesthetic delight the flames that were consuming his ill-fated capital. Such was the retreat chosen by Maecenas, when he obtained the emperor's permission to retire from public life and to seek what Tacitus calls a sort of *peregrinum otium* within the city. Here he entertained the poets to whom he owes most of

[1] Hor., *Od.* iii. 29.   [2] Pliny, *Hist. Nat.* vii. 52.
[3] Sen.; *De Prov.* iii. 9.

his fame, and here he held close intercourse with the pure spirit of Virgil, to whom he had presented a house on the Esquiline close to his own. Augustus, in one of the pleasant letters to him happily preserved to us by Suetonius, declares his wish to steal from him Horace, whom he desires to engage as a private secretary. ' *Veniet ergo,*' he writes, ' *ab ista parasitica mensa ad hanc regiam, et nos in scribendis epistolis juvabit*' ('Let him quit that parasitic table of yours for our palace, and he shall help us with our correspondence'[1]). But Horace declined the proposal; and Augustus, ever reasonable, had the good sense not to be offended. Both Horace and Virgil, however, much preferred the country to the town, and their patron, sorely against his will, was obliged to indulge their inclinations in this respect.

Maecenas had evidently a genius for friendship. We read that a certain Melissus, a distinguished grammarian, although free-born, had been exposed in his infancy by his mother and brought up as a slave. He became of the household of Maecenas, and was by him treated rather as a friend than as a servant. Afterwards, his mother, repenting of her action, claimed him as her son, and he was thus given the opportunity of recovering his freedom. But, preferring to liberty his actual condition in the service of Maecenas, he rejected the proffered acknowledgment. He was afterwards manumitted by Maecenas, introduced to the emperor, and appointed librarian to the new Octavian Library.[2]

---

[1] Suet., *in vita Hor.*   [2] Suet.; *De Illus. Gramm.* 21.

It is often the case with men whose friendship
is valuable and enduring that their manner in
the early stages of acquaintance shows a certain
tentative reserve. The plant of genuine affection
between male friends is apt to be of slow growth.
Maecenas was no exception to this rule. Horace
tells us that when he was first introduced to
Maecenas, to whom he was recommended by
Virgil, he was received rather coldly and not
recalled for nine months. But from that time
onwards there seems to have been no break in a
mutual sympathy that ever increased. As a
friend Maecenas was no respecter of persons.
With the emperor he used a freedom which he
permitted to those who were more or less depen-
dent on himself. The well-known story of how,
when Augustus was sitting at the seat of justice
and about to condemn many men to death,
Maecenas, unable from the press to approach him,
threw to him a little scroll with ' *Surge tandem
carnifex*ᵃ ('Rise, hangman!') written on it, and
how the emperor at once rose and left the tribunal without another word, is equally credit-
able to both these friends. The lives of the
accused were spared, and the bold minister
gained rather than lost credit with his master.[1]
Nor did he lose his favour when, by his indiscretion in confiding to his wife Terentia the secret
of the discovery of Murena's conspiracy, he risked
the failure of the measures taken for its suppres-
sion. To his own dependents he extended the
indulgence received by him from the emperor.

[1] Dion Cassius, iv. 7.

He was not offended when Horace broke his promise of returning to Rome, and lingered month after month first in his Sabine farm and afterwards, during the winter months, on the southern coast. The poetic apology he earned from him would, it is true, have soothed the indignation of most men. '*Horati Flacci, ut mei, memor esto*' ('Remember Horace as you would myself'), was his last testamentary recommendation to the emperor.[1] Horace did not long survive him, and was buried on the Esquiline close to his patron's grave.

The patience of Maecenas was tried by the rather feeble character of Propertius, and he used often to urge that poet to quit his lovelorn ditties and compose something more worthy of his talents. Propertius replied by citing his patron's moderation in remaining a knight as an example to others to confine themselves within modest spheres of action.[2] Virgil was an even older friend than Horace, but his shyness and taciturnity probably rendered their relations less easy and unreserved. In the anonymous biography of Virgil which has descended to us from ancient times there are two replies made by the poet to the minister which one would fain believe to be authentic. On one occasion he was asked by Maecenas, characteristically enough, ' Is there anything, Virgil, that man can possess without satiety ? ' ' In everything,' was the reply, ' staleness or abundance produces disgust—except in understanding.' At another time Maecenas

[1] Suet., *in vita Hor.*   [2] Prop. iii. 9.

asked him in what manner it was profitable to enjoy and preserve great gifts of fortune. Virgil replied : ' Then only when a man is ambitious to surpass others as greatly in justice and liberality as he does in wealth and honours.'

Maecenas was a copious author, but he probably did not attach much importance to his own compositions. It is remarkable that among all the compliments showered upon him by his *parasitica mensa*—by Horace, Virgil, and Propertius —not one relates to his literary productions, and it is a fair inference that his vanity was not much interested in their success. He was as indifferent to the literary as he was to the political traditions of Rome. The *nova elocutio* which he introduced into his poetry, the transpositions of words from their natural places for the sake of effect, the preciosities of his style, were derided by his contemporaries, and cited by later critics like Seneca and Quintilian as the classical examples of this kind of vicious composition.[1] The few specimens of his poetry that have descended to us abundantly bear out the charge, though it must be remembered that, for the most part, they are expressly cited with that object. The severe taste of Augustus, who equally disliked the affected imitation of old writers by the use of obsolete words, and the over-ornate and eccentric manner of the new school, did not spare the euphemisms and quaintnesses of the minister's style. Macrobius has preserved for us the end of a letter from the emperor to Maecenas in

[1] Sen., *Ep.* 19, 114 ; Quint. ix. 4.

which he parodies his friend's style with happy effect: '*Vale mel gentium,*' so it runs, '*melcule, ebur ex Hetruria, laver Aretinum, adamas supernus, Tiberinum margaritum, Cilniorum smaragde, jaspis figulorum, berylle Porsennae, carbunculum Italiae.*' [1] Maecenas's love of precious stones, of which we have evidence in some surviving hendecasyllables addressed by him to Horace, is also rallied in this letter. Seneca, to whom we owe much of our scanty knowledge of Maecenas, tells us that his writings were often great in their meaning, but enervated by their expression. [2]

The change effected in the Roman character at the close of the first century before Christ, with its subsequent developments, offers an interesting study to the philosophic historian. The house was completed, the architects who had superintended its completion had fought for its possession, into which the strongest of them had finally entered. The employment which had absorbed the lives of the workmen was at an end, and now their unemployed descendants began to look about them and to wonder what they were to do next. In fact, the cultivated Romans, having for the first time leisure to remember that they were alive, began the dangerous search for theories of life. Philosophy, which, as we learn from Cicero, was still in his time by many considered a study below the dignity of a Roman gentleman, now began powerfully to attract the attention of the educated classes, and the writings of the Greek philosophers were eagerly discussed. Stoicism,

[1] Mac., *Sat.* ii. 4   [2] *Ep.* 92.

with its seeming paradoxes, appealed very little at first to the downright Roman mind. A love of the palpable and a contempt for subtlety were among its prominent characteristics. The *via media* of the Peripatetics found more favour, but men in search of a new belief do not readily adopt compromises, which spring from the attempt to adapt to new conditions an old creed that we are loth to desert. But Epicureanism, which professed to base itself upon common sense and the direct testimony of the senses, and which swept impatiently away the whole paraphernalia of logic with its definitions and distinctions, progressed with amazing rapidity. Bodily pleasure, cried the Epicureans, is the ultimate good ; and a respectable life is to be recommended, because without it bodily pleasure becomes impossible. Pain is the only real evil ; other so-called ills are the artificial creations of opinion. The foolish are tossed to and fro on the phantasmal waves of hopes and fears ; let them pull themselves together and shake off the dream, and they will find themselves on dry land. By the study of unsophisticated beasts we may see nature as in a mirror ; let us imitate them, and no longer groan under the tyranny of convention. The opposite of pain is exemption from pain, and this is the highest enduring pleasure. Pain must often be endured and even courted in order to avoid a future greater pain, and pleasure sacrificed to the attainment of a future greater pleasure. To attain these objects courage is a useful and temperance an essential quality. As objects in space appear

smaller or larger as they are nearer or more distant,
so do pleasures and pains in time. The function
of wisdom is to estimate their real magnitude,
and to correct by reason the errors induced by
the fallacious aspect which they offer to the
passions. The accessories of pleasure and pain
rather than the things themselves excite our hopes
and fears ; by philosophy these accessories will
be made to vanish, and the two objects—which
alone have a real existence—will be regarded in
their own naked proportions. Providence is a
myth ; the combination of atoms, which in
infinite time has formed man, is fortuitous ;
there is a continual passage of elements into
things and of things into elements ; the world
and all that therein is are things, and therefore
mortal ; nothing endures but the atoms of which
the number of shapes is limited, while in each
shape the number of atoms is infinite.

Though the contradictions and poverties involved in this system were ably exposed by Cicero
in his book *De Finibus*, yet the tenets continued
to spread, and deeply affected the Roman character and history. Liberty now seemed an unsub-
stantial notion, an empty name, for which it was
the height of absurdity to suffer. Alone among
philosophers the Epicurean lecturers never alluded
in their discourses to the ancient heroes of Greece
and Rome. Atticus is a good specimen of the
best class of men who at this time adopted Epicureanism. Living in accordance with his principles
in retirement at Athens, where his amiability
made him the idol of the people, he remained

throughout his life on the best terms with the various party-leaders, nor did the assassination of his friends appear to him a sufficient reason for quarrelling with their assassins. Sylla and Pompey, Marcus Brutus and Julius Caesar, Cicero and Antony, and finally Octavius, were all included in the list of his friends.

> *Suave etiam belli. certamina magna tueri*
> *Per campos instructa tua sine parte pericli.*

Consistent to the end, he deliberately starved himself to death in order to avoid the greater pain of a lingering illness. The civil wars must have appeared to him a melancholy absurdity, useful only as they placed in more striking relief his own philosophical tranquillity.

It is not difficult to account for the rapid spread of the new philosophy among the Roman upper classes. The miseries of the civil wars gave reason to those who asserted their irrationality. The contrast between the tangible enjoyments possible under the strong imperial government and the pains which were endured while Brutus and Cato were still struggling for an idea was made and registered by the practical Roman mind. The Emperor Augustus, who regarded life as a sorry play in which he was amused to find that the principal part had fallen to himself, Augustus, with his sceptical good sense and moderation, encouraged to some extent the ideas which afforded so effective a guarantee for the stability of his government, though at times he was alarmed at the progress they had made and endeavoured to check them by precept and example.

And his minister, Maecenas, found ready to his hand a theory of life which exactly accorded with his own inclinations and habits of mind. Cultured, luxurious, and good-natured, he disliked stiffness, whether in manners, literature, or dress. He was himself of noble birth, but believed the distinctions of rank to be the creations of an empty convention. His enjoyment of the pleasures of life has seldom been rivalled, and his main departure from the principles of his school lay in his consequent horror of death. He was a man of great intellect, of an exquisite taste in literature, and there was probably no affectation in his laughing disregard of all the old Roman conventions. Such was Maecenas; and great indeed must have been the change which had passed over the genius of the Roman Commonwealth when such a man could appear at its head.

APPENDIX

TABLE I

Augustus Imp. = (1) Claudia, (2) Scribonia, (3) Livia

Julia = (1) Marcellus, (2) M. Agrippa, (3) Tiberius

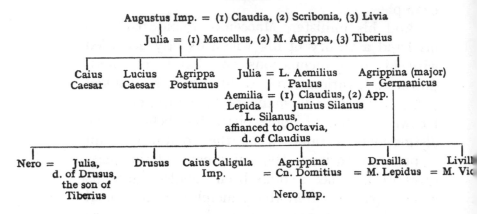

| Caius Caesar | Lucius Caesar | Agrippa Postumus | Julia = L. Aemilius Paulus
Aemilia = (1) Claudius, (2) App.
Lepida \| Junius Silanus
L. Silanus,
affianced to Octavia,
d. of Claudius | Agrippina (major) = Germanicus |

| Nero = Julia, d. of Drusus, the son of Tiberius | Drusus | Caius Caligula Imp. | Agrippina = Cn. Domitius
Nero Imp. | Drusilla = M. Lepidus | Livill = M. Vic |

TABLE II

Livia Drusilla = (1) Tiberius Claudius Nero, (2) Augustus

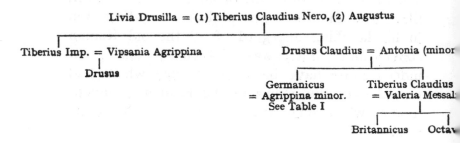

| Tiberius Imp. = Vipsania Agrippina
Drusus | Drusus Claudius = Antonia (minor |

| Germanicus = Agrippina minor. See Table I | Tiberius Claudius = Valeria Messal |

| Britannicus | Octa\ |

TABLE III

Marcus Annaeus Seneca = Helvia

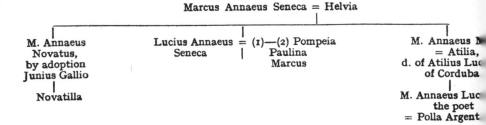

| M. Annaeus Novatus, by adoption Junius Gallio
Novatilla | Lucius Annaeus = (1)—(2) Pompeia Seneca \| Paulina Marcus | M. Annaeus N = Atilia, d. of Atilius Luc of Corduba
M. Annaeus Luc the poet = Polla Argent |